CREATIVE
ROOM STYLES

Room-by-room guide to home decor

CREATIVE
PUBLISHING
international

Minnetonka, Minnesota

D1307014

Table *of* Contents

Bedrooms

Halls and Baths

CHOOSING A COLOR SCHEME

Design your room the professional way by collecting samples and swatches that match and contrast – it can be real fun, and will instill even the most timid home decorator with confidence.

Setting the Mood

Take time to think how you want the room to *feel* – the mood that you want to create. Color, texture and pattern can all strongly influence the atmosphere of a room, and you can use them to set the scene for your daily living, rather like a set designer on a stage.

For example, warm, glowing berry reds, soft, fuzzy textures such as wool and chenille, and traditional, flowing patterns blend together to give a welcoming, cozy effect; gleaming chintzes in pale pastels, combined with marble or stone accessories, and sparkling glass chandeliers create a sense of cool elegance.

An hour or two spent browsing through books and magazines may help you to define your ideas more clearly. Look for pictures that catch the feel of the room you want – not necessarily an interior scene. A spectacular sunset in a travel brochure may hint at a Dramatic color scheme in red and gold with theatrical lighting; a burst of cornflowers or delphiniums in a seed catalog could lead you toward a medley of blue floral patterns for a Country Cottage scheme; or a book of antique engravings may inspire a Classic room scheme featuring architectural prints on cool, neutral walls.

Keeping color and tone in close harmony – as with these muted shades of russet, apricot and soft green – means you can blend together a variety of patterns to create a restful but satisfying room scheme.

5

Pattern Combinations

You don't have to stick to just one pattern per room – in fact, this can result in a flat, lifeless effect. A few simple rules will help you mix various patterns for satisfying but natural-looking results.

Linking colors

Different patterns on walls, fabrics and furniture can blend harmoniously if the same colorway flows through them all. This is the basic rule used for many coordinated collections.

The newest coordinates cover every decorating eventuality, from basics such as fabrics, wallpaper, paint and tiles to accessories such as bed linen and lamp shades. Many carry coordination through to matching ceramics.

A fully integrated package of solids and patterns offers an enormous range of decorative possibilities. You may use as many elements as you wish to achieve a completely matched finish. Alternatively, you can take a more selective approach, omitting entire pattern themes or changing the proportion of the patterns to tilt the balance toward a particular style.

A sample collection illustrates the adaptability of these coordinates in the rooms shown opposite. It offers a strong floral pattern that carries a visual index of all the colors in the rest of the collection.

Typical supplements to the main pattern are color-matched geometrics or solids, in this case a checked fabric, striped wallpaper and a deep pink textured fabric. Paint in two shades of pink and a neutral beige is also used.

The strong floral design is picked out again in ready-made accessories including a blind, tiebacks and picture frames.

Linking patterns

You can mix the same magic by using a pattern as a coordinating link throughout the room, rather than color. Try a wallpaper with a subtle neutral stripe as a background, then use different widths of stripe in two or three stronger colors, in other areas. The strict linear design sets up a rhythm of pattern around the room that even powerful contrasts such as reds and greens can't disturb. A mixed group of checked pillows on a sofa works in the same way.

Main pattern focus

Choose one strong pattern as the focus for the room. Pick out individual colors from it, and look for smaller or less forceful patterns that feature one or two of the colors – a tiny overall print, maybe, or diminutive checks and fancy stripes. Dashes of other colors may enter the scheme in this way, but as long as none of the patterns rival the main one for attention they will simply add to the general warmth and liveliness. Pull out plain colors from the focus pattern to use for paintwork and accents – piping around cushions, lamp shades and trimming details.

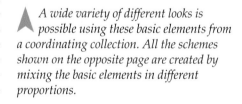 *A wide variety of different looks is possible using these basic elements from a coordinating collection. All the schemes shown on the opposite page are created by mixing the basic elements in different proportions.*

To go with many coordinating fabrics, paints and wallcoverings, there is a range of ready-made accessories to match, from lamp shades and picture frames to covered boxes – or you can make your own.

With the emphasis on the showy floral fabric and refined pink stripe wallpaper, the room emerges with a quietly romantic feel. The floral curtains are draped softly to echo the curved motifs on the fabric and the rounded shape of the armchair. Tying back full-length curtains high like this accentuates the height of the window, reinforcing the effect of the striped walls.

Here, checks and stripes predominate, with the bold floral playing a supporting role on the roller blind, over the dado and as lining and tiebacks for the curtains. Small touches of plain fabric on the pillows, and the paintwork on the skirting board anchor the mixture of patterns.

In this version of the look, the floral holds the center stage at the window while the picture-rail-height floral border and pillows disperse the traditional theme around the room. Color-linked, low-key checks and plain pink walls soften the bold floral pattern.

Gathering Samples

The best way to arrive at a pleasing combination of all the different components, such as wallpaper, fabric and carpet, is to collect samples, or cuttings, to take home and mull over. Collecting samples means you can plan the complete scheme before you pick up your paintbrush, and avoid costly mistakes.

Wall and floors Some stores are more helpful about samples than others. DIY stores have a huge range of paint colors, and supply card strips for you to take away. If you are nervous about a color, you may find a sample can so you can try it out on a small patch of wall. Wallpaper and border samples are usually not difficult to obtain, but you need a big enough piece to see the effect from a distance as well as at close range.

If you can't get floorcovering samples, look for promotional leaflets showing colors and patterns. Some companies have small 'tufts' available for you to borrow.

Fabrics Some fabric stores will give you only a narrow strip of fabric. For an accurate impression of how a pattern will relate to the room and to other patterns, you may choose to purchase a small sample. For large patterns, some companies supply a larger returnable sample, which you can keep for a month before receiving a bill. It's useful to make a note of pattern repeats, fabric widths and prices so you can bear in mind the quantities and costs when choosing at home.

Details Don't forget minor details such as small accessories and trimmings – a snippet of fringe to pick out the edge of a cushion, or a piece of ribbon for a picture bow. Touches of color like these help to round off the effect, and it's a good idea to include them at this stage.

Collect as wide a selection of samples as possible so that you have plenty of alternatives to choose from.

Country

▲ *Floral prints mix happily with linen and plain cotton in a typical Country scheme. Delicate lace and finely striped fabrics add freshness. Neutral carpets and warm-toned wooden furniture complete the look.*

Contemporary

◄ *Functional simplicity is the keynote in a Contemporary scheme. Choose pastel colors, neutral shades and gentle patterns to provide an easygoing background. This gives you the opportunity to add stronger color accents for soft furnishings and accessories.*

A SAMPLE BOARD

When you have collected a range of samples, spend some time sorting through and narrowing down your choice to a few favorites, checking that they go well together and also in the actual room itself. The professional way to finalize the scheme is to make a sample board. This means putting together your chosen samples, together with a sketch or photo if you wish, arranged so that you can see the way each pattern or color relates to the others around the room. Find a large board and arrange your samples on it. Overlap one or two if they are going to be closely related in the room – fabrics for sofa and pillows, for instance – or to make an attractive grouping. Pleat a curtain sample into a pretty fan to simulate the folds of the curtain. Once you are happy with the arrangement, glue all the pieces down. Prop the board up in the room for a few days, to acclimatize yourself to the scheme.

Other ideas may spring to mind, and you can easily make changes, or even alternative schemes, at this stage, so that when you do make a start, you will be confident of the end result.

Classic

▼ *Grace and comfort are essential elements of the Classic look. Plain or discreetly patterned walls are the perfect foil for floral and leafy chintz and richly patterned damask. This formal look is reinforced by gilded picture frames and mirrors.*

Dramatic

▶ Lavish colors and rich textures combine with the luster of faded gilt or the stark Gothic look of cast iron for a Dramatic room with impact and individuality. Recreate the myths of the past with medieval motifs and royal purple, or set a stage of theatrical grandeur with silks and fake furs – the look is big, bold and beautiful.

Ethnic

◀ Create an Exotic scheme with a treasure trove of colorful patterns. Spicy colors and handcrafted textiles complement solid wooden furniture and natural floorcoverings. Oriental designs can be mixed with paisley shawls, hand-printed cotton throws or distinctive Eastern embroidery.

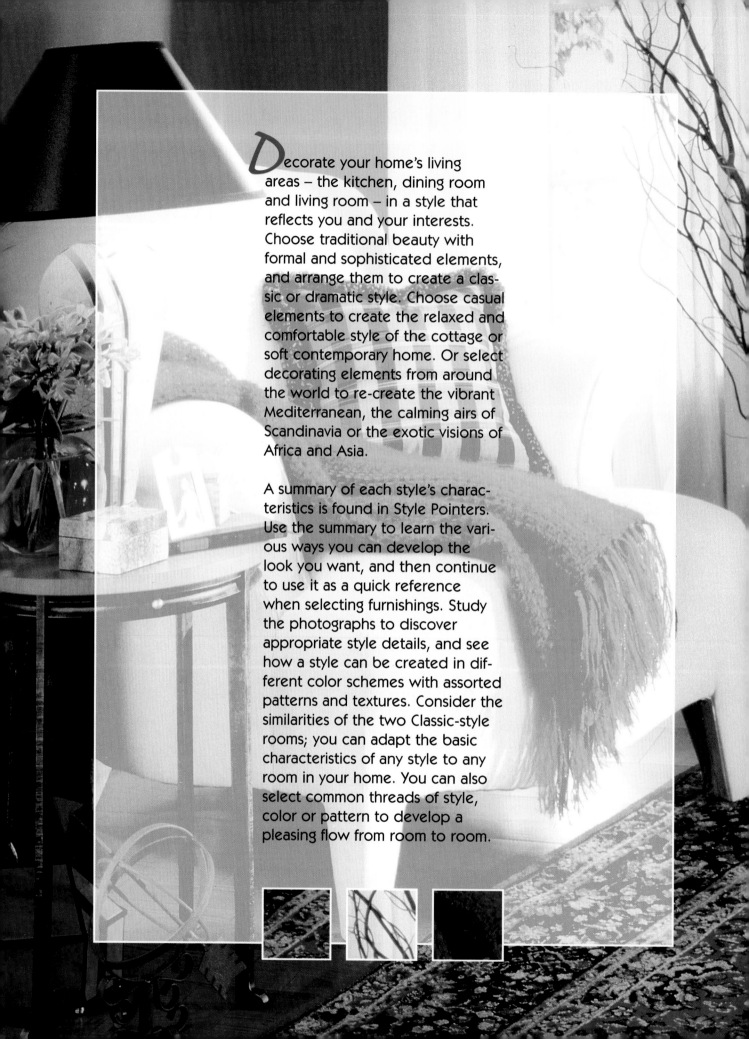

Decorate your home's living areas – the kitchen, dining room and living room – in a style that reflects you and your interests. Choose traditional beauty with formal and sophisticated elements, and arrange them to create a classic or dramatic style. Choose casual elements to create the relaxed and comfortable style of the cottage or soft contemporary home. Or select decorating elements from around the world to re-create the vibrant Mediterranean, the calming airs of Scandinavia or the exotic visions of Africa and Asia.

A summary of each style's characteristics is found in Style Pointers. Use the summary to learn the various ways you can develop the look you want, and then continue to use it as a quick reference when selecting furnishings. Study the photographs to discover appropriate style details, and see how a style can be created in different color schemes with assorted patterns and textures. Consider the similarities of the two Classic-style rooms; you can adapt the basic characteristics of any style to any room in your home. You can also select common threads of style, color or pattern to develop a pleasing flow from room to room.

CLASSIC KITCHEN

*Craftsmanship and traditional materials create the discreetly smart
and practical Classic kitchen. Colors are light and low-key, and
details reflect a penchant for quality and period style.*

The Classic kitchen is as functional and well planned as any high-tech, modern equivalent, but its appearance is practical and stylish in a softer, more subtle way. First impressions are of a light and airy room, where details are elegant yet restrained. Even in very limited space, the well-proportioned fittings seem to blend easily with the surrounding decor – a feature that owes much to a pale color scheme and uncluttered layout. The look is equally successful in a period home or modern apartment, and works well in open-plan schemes, where its sophisticated styling is at ease near a dining or living room area.

Buttermilk cream and a hand-painted look are typical of the Classic kitchen, as are professional pans and utensils. The influence of traditional carpentry skills is evident in the plate rack and paneling details.

A sense of custom-made craftsmanship is evident in the paneled doors, detailed moldings and fretwork trims associated with Classic style. Whether the kitchen units are in pale wood such as maple or limed oak, or painted in a typical cream color, the time-honored skills of the cabinetmaker are evident in the finished effect.

13

CREATING THE STYLE

At first glance, a Classic kitchen is not unlike other traditional styles; what makes it different is its feeling of lightness and its definitive emphasis on classical proportions and decorative detail. Largely based on the ambience of the comfortable and practical kitchens in the affluent homes of the past, elements of the Classic kitchen are borrowed mostly from grand country or Colonial homes and Georgian and Regency town houses.

In the more formal of the kitchen variations, you can see classical influences in carved pillars, pediments and arches, and railing-like fretwork galleries across the tops of cabinet units. In most versions, there are neat runs of dentil block molding beneath cornice trims, and typically, glazed unit doors are divided into tall, narrow panes and fitted with beveled glass. The most exclusive Classic kitchens are in solid pale woods such as maple, ash, beech or limed oak, but the equally characteristic, colored versions, now made from MDF (medium-density fiberboard), are painted in a stippled, dragged or antique crackle effect, with paneling highlighted in a subtle color contrast and with toning wood or ceramic knobs.

Create a spacious feel with a wall color that is in harmony with the units – use either plain paint, or a wallcovering with a subtle self-color stripe, check or small motif. Any contrast color should be a muted, 'historic' color, or a warm earth pigment or a spicy shade.

Choose black-and-white check flooring to copy traditional marble, a stone effect, woodblock or old, stripped and polished floorboards for a mellow look.

STYLE POINTERS

 WALLS Plain/discreet pattern: pale and mid-tone paint; wallcovering with small, stylized motifs or stripes.
Tiles: Plain squares, white or pale with low-key contrast borders or Delft-style inserts; hand-painted tiles.

 WINDOWS Formal: tailored, lined curtains with cornice or formal pleated valance or heading; draped swags.
Blinds: ruched Austrian or shaped-edge roller blinds.

 FLOORING Tiles/boards: quarry tiles, flagstone effects; black-and-white checkered effect; stained/polished floorboards.

 FABRICS Traditional/natural: cotton and chintz florals; stylized theme patterns; formal checks and stripes.

 FURNITURE Finely crafted: built-in and freestanding units; cream/pale hand-painted wood/MDF (medium-density fiberboard); maple, ash, beech, limed pine or oak; period detailing and moldings; Georgian-style glazed/paneled doors; woodblock, marble/Corian®, white tile worktops; painted wood/ceramic knobs, period-style pewter or iron swing handles.
Kitchen table and chairs: turned-leg/pedestal period styles; lacquered cane; formal styles; chairs with tailored removable cushions, overstuffed/drop-in upholstered seats.
Appliances: solid-fuel stove; modern built-in oven and appliances hidden by paneled housings; traditional sink or Corian®/marble styles; woodblock or marble worktops.

 LIGHTING Practical/formal: discreet, halogen ceiling spots, period-style glass or lantern pendant fitting.

 ACCESSORIES Traditional/period style: period brass/chrome faucets, professional stainless steel and copper pans and utensils; wooden plate rack; classic-pattern china; mason-style glass storage jars, stoneware jars.

Cream-painted units with fretwork and cornice moldings are typical features of the Classic kitchen. *Georgian-style glazing,* with its classical proportions, is an integral part of the style. *A white ceramic tiled floor* is laid in a traditional pattern, and creates a spacious effect. *High-back cane chairs* feature an elegant trellis design with classical origins. *A valance and tiebacks* are typical Classic style touches.

In the Classic kitchen, discreet paneled housing hides modern appliances such as a refrigerator or dishwasher. In this sophisticated, blond wood kitchen, the influence of classical architecture is very evident in the elegant central pediment detailing and the geometric floor design.

15

Cream-painted units incorporate key Classic style elements: a traditional solid-fuel stove – note the built-in microwave alongside – and a fitted dish rack above the butler sink. A warming brick red wallcovering makes the large room cozy, and balances the rich timber floor color.

The elements of the style are all here in this relaxed version of the Classic kitchen. A handsome custom-made hutch boasts pillars and fretwork detailing, and sets off the traditional blue-and-white china display. An antique chair and period prints complete the look.

CLASSIC KITCHEN FURNISHINGS

Special open shelving units, painted to match other units or to match the wall color, are in keeping with the style, as is a focal-point hutch with elegant proportions in polished wood. Use this to display period-style china – classic blue-and-white, or dainty floral china, as well as functional white porcelain.

Window treatments should be smart and practical – in either plain colors or in a classic floral print. Use a simple, shaped-edge roller blind, pleated blind or Austrian blind at a small window. Or, for a kitchen that is used as a dining area too, team a blind with a more formal window treatment such as curtains and a valance, fabric-covered cornice or swag and tails, as appropriate.

If space permits, a table and chairs can be "borrowed" from a Classic dining room. A small fruitwood pedestal table and period chairs look elegant and are in keeping with the look, as is a sophisticated, pale lacquered cane and glass table and chairs. Alternatively, cover a more basic table with a traditional damask cloth, or with a plain or print fabric to coordinate with the window treatment.

▼ *A subtle crackle paint effect helps to blend an essential electrical appliance with the cupboard units in this kitchen, where old and new collectibles merge comfortably.*

▲ *Typical of Classic style, the maple hutch, with its beautifully crafted paneling and ornate pewter handles, looks elegant and understated in a simple setting.*

◄ *To capture something of the elegance of this period home in a modern kitchen, choose a calming, pale color scheme for basic units; team these with warm, wooden worksurfaces and floor; then add a floral ruched blind in colors to highlight a simple display of china plates.*

STYLE DETAILS

Traditional kitchen equipment is naturally at home in the Classic kitchen. Cooking utensils are functional – no frills or unnecessary pattern, and no gimmicks. Modern plastic appliances are a part of modern life, but for a low-key period look, choose a stainless steel kettle and toaster, professional-style saucepans, utensils and storage canisters. Accessorize with a white enameled or stoneware bread box, a porcelain cheese dome or wire mesh cheese safe, and old-fashioned glass jars, wooden boards and platters. An integral wooden plate rack and towel rail are very much a part of the style, as are cast-iron skillets and a freestanding saucepan rack. Display fruit or vegetables lavishly in a large, period-style china dish, in a wooden bowl or on a brass, copper or pewter platter. For a really grand effect, make an arrangement in a stone pedestal urn – you could look for one in a garden center.

▲ *A favorite for centuries, blue-and-white china is a design classic, and entirely in keeping with the traditional look of a Classic-style kitchen.*

► *With its cream coloring, ornate hinges and shapely posts, this little wire-fronted cheese or egg safe is a typical Classic style accessory.*

▲ *Period-style faucets are an important design detail, as are flower and plant displays – and ivy is a Classic choice for a window box.*

▲ *Convert an alcove into a classic dresser with wallcovering border or cutouts. Surround it with shapely molding, and add paneled doors and a real china collection to complete the effect.*

◄ *The hallmark of custom-made carpentry is attention to detail. Here, a traditional towel rail fits discreetly into a small recess in this attractive limed wood kitchen.*

MEDITERRANEAN KITCHEN

Informal and vibrant, the Mediterranean kitchen is the heart of the home. Create this rustic – yet essentially practical – style, using sun-drenched color, natural materials and hand-painted pottery.

Chunky crockery, painted in warm earthy colors, soft furnishings in busy mix-and-match patterns, ropes of onions and jars of herb vinegars and oils all help create an authentic Mediterranean feel in the kitchen.

The warm and welcoming Mediterranean kitchen is a hive of culinary activity; all the elements linked to the preparation and enjoyment of food are prominently displayed here. Aromatic herbs and oils, bowls and baskets of fruit and vegetables, and a battery of well-used cooking utensils and richly glazed earthenware pots take pride of place against a rustic backdrop. Rough-plastered walls, stone or tiled floors, weathered timber doors, shuttered windows, simple, sturdy wooden furniture and colorful soft furnishings set the scene.

You may not have a sunny kitchen or a rustic home, but you can easily create a Mediterranean atmosphere in your kitchen with color and texture, and by introducing a few readily available key accessories.

CREATING THE STYLE

Aspects of Mediterranean style vary in a subtle way from west to east, and may embrace rustic, rural or coastal overtones. Throughout, a vibrant use of colors such as royal blue, saffron yellow, olive green, crimson, dusky pink, clear white and the earthy colors of brick red and ochre predominate – on tiles, fabrics and pottery, and in more muted tones for painted wooden furniture.

In the western part of the Mediterranean you may take inspiration from the distinctive mini-print fabrics and richly glazed ceramics of Provence to create the well-loved Provençal style or, for a more rustic effect, look east towards the Greek islands with their pebble mosaics and traditional embroidered linens. Here, simplicity and the dramatic contrast of white walls set against the vibrant blue of sea and sky can be an energizing starting point for a bold and basic kitchen scheme.

Whichever influence you choose, color is central to achieving the Mediterranean look; this, plus a few distinctive fabrics used for table linens or curtains, and a small selection of regional pottery will give more than a hint of the style, leaving you to make as subtle or bold a statement as you wish. Whichever approach you choose, try to include a solid wooden table in the kitchen, as this provides an informal focal point.

STYLE POINTERS

 WALLS Rough plaster: create a rustic finish with textured paint; or flat white paint with wide contrast border around windows and doors; or colorwash in a pale shade for an aged effect; combine with flat painted woodwork in subtle Mediterranean colors.
Wall tiles: vibrant; plain or patterned blue, yellow, ochre, green and deep red; place square or diagonally as splashbacks.

 WINDOWS Shutters/café curtains: internal louvered wood shutters in traditional flat finish green or dusty brown; café curtains in Provençal prints or white cotton crocheted/embroidered linen; simple roller, slatted wood or Roman blinds.
Window boxes: terra-cotta/weathered wood for geraniums or herbs.

 FLOORING Slabs/tiles/stripped wood: rustic stone slabs, terra-cotta or black-and-white tiles, plain or with border patterns. Create the effect with vinyl floorcovering. Stain stripped boards for an authentic-looking aged finish.

 FABRICS Provençal prints/embroidery: colorful Provençal prints for curtains, blinds and table linen; or embroidery in bold black, brown or red cross-stitch on linen; or white crocheted lace pieces.

 FURNITURE Rustic wood: walnut, chestnut, olive, pine; use color stain or weathered paint effects – soft white, deep blue, olive green, with contrast lines and details.
Kitchen table and chairs: large pine table and chairs; traditional, painted ladderback chairs with rush seats or Provençal print cushions and table linen.

 LIGHTING Focused on activity: a pendant metal shade or chandelier over the kitchen table; ceramic or metal lanterns, candle sconces; illuminate work surfaces with discreetly placed strip lights.

ACCESSORIES Rustic, natural: hand-painted terra-cotta tableware; rustic glassware, pitchers, bowls, plates; cast-iron and aluminium pans, baskets, olive wood bowls; Provençal-print and embroidered table linen/cushions.
Flowers: geraniums, sunflowers.
Food, fruits and herbs: jars of pasta, olives, garlic braids, onion strings; bowls of lemons, limes and oranges; Mediterranean herbs: rosemary, thyme, sage, basil, oregano and mint add color and an authentic aroma.

▼ *Vibrant, yet muted paint colors for walls and kitchen units evoke all the warmth of the Mediterranean. Little splashes of local color – a bowl of oranges, bright, hand-painted pottery and fresh, green vegetables – add to the evocative atmosphere.*

▲ **Contrast molding trims** on painted wooden units are
typical details in the rustic Mediterranean kitchen.
Terra-cotta tiles, with their warm, earthy tones, are the
traditional, hard-wearing choice for flooring.
A decorative pendant light placed centrally over the table
creates an intimate atmosphere for Mediterranean kitchen dining.
Handsome containers, cooking utensils and ingredients on
prominent display are a key element of Mediterranean style.

21

MEDITERRANEAN FURNISHINGS

Storage units in the Mediterranean kitchen are both decorative and practical. Traditionally, there is a handsome antique armoire or corner cupboard, often with doors left permanently open to reveal a colorful display of pottery, tableware and glass. If space permits, you can recreate this effect using a stripped pine cupboard or wardrobe fitted with shelves, and use it to link a dining area or to extend the kitchen into a corridor. Alternatively, fill a rustic pine hutch or shelves with a collection of Mediterranean pottery.

If you have a standard fitted kitchen, dark-stained wood will give a traditional Mediterranean look. You can add beading and fretwork molding trim for a rustic twist on plain cupboards and shelves, or paint the units a flat Mediterranean hue, and highlight any relief details in a contrast color. For an authentic look, edge shelves or back glass-paneled doors with Provençal prints, embroidered linen or crocheted fabrics.

Freestanding stoves are traditional, but modern built-in appliances are a practical way of life, and they blend quite happily with the style, particularly in classic white.

A pine kitchen table can double as a work surface, especially if it has a tiled center panel. The chairs can match, or you can combine different rustic shapes, linking them with coordinating seat cushions or by painting them in matching or toning colors.

A rough-textured plaster finish evokes rustic, Mediterranean walls, and sunny yellow complements the effect. A painted ladder-back chair, a patchwork tablecloth in Provençal fabrics and a jug of sunflowers all add distinctive style notes.

Mediterranean pitchers have an earthy practicality and distinctive shape that makes for easy pouring.

◀ *Extravagant scrolls and curls decorate this handsome painted armoire. Cupboards of this style are often the focal point of Mediterranean kitchens and are used, as here, to display an impressive ceramic collection.*

▶ *No Mediterranean style kitchen would seem complete without a few pieces of its hallmark hand-painted pottery. Here, its vibrant colors are echoed in the charming patterns of the Provençal print fabrics.*

▼ *Glossy tiles set in a diagonal pattern are a traditional feature in Mediterranean kitchens. In this kitchen, fresh green and white provide the color theme, which is carried through to glass and ceramic accessories.*

▼ *Store pasta in airtight jars and trim with raffia ties for a stylish Mediterranean look.*

STYLE DETAILS

The Mediterranean-style kitchen has many distinctive features to draw on – those little details, both culinary and colorful, that epitomize the style so that even the smallest addition suggests its lively atmosphere.

Since the Mediterranean kitchen is very much a working kitchen, capture its character with a hanging display of essentials – cooking pots, utensils, strings of onions, garlic braids and herbs all add local color. For a style accent, and to add a color splash to a table or worktop, use a hand-painted tile or two as pot stands. Fill shelves with rustic pottery and Mediterranean foods, bottled oils and herbal vinegars. All are relatively easy to find and instantly set the mood.

▲ *Introduce Mediterranean-style detailing to a mellow pine cupboard with a collection of rustic pottery and a decorative rail edging.*

▲ *Oregano, sage, parsley and thyme are favorite Mediterranean herbs. Keep them at hand in a terra-cotta window box to add authentic flavor to your cooking.*

▲ *Use Mediterranean herbs to flavor cooking oils and vinegars, then cork them in an assortment of eye-catching glass bottles.*

► *Provençal prints reflect all the color and vivacity of Mediterranean style. Accessories in these delightful patterned fabrics are guaranteed to add a touch of joie de vivre to your kitchen.*

CLASSIC DINING ROOM

Create a graceful setting for family gatherings and formal dinners – the Classic dining room is elegantly inviting and richly embellished with the traditional furnishings and accessories of the past.

Sophisticated but welcoming, Classic style makes an elegant choice for a dining room, bringing a sense of the gracious living and refinement of a previous era. It is not a difficult or expensive style to achieve, and you don't need to live in a period home to re-create the look. You can add architectural moldings such as cornicing and a central ceiling rose to a plain modern room, and choose reproduction furniture to create a period feel. Revamped junk-shop finds – an old picture frame sprayed gold, large china platters to hang on the wall, or odd pieces of silver plate – give that unique, distinctive, Classic look.

The rich colors of russet and burnt orange create a warm, inviting atmosphere in these Classic dining room settings. Once the table is laid, the soft glow of candlelight completes the mood.

CREATING THE STYLE

The Classic dining room has a formal, rather than a functional look, designed to impress. Aim for a feeling of spaciousness, with a pale ceiling to give an impression of height, and sweeping floor-length curtains. If the room is a reasonable size, follow a well-used tradition and choose a strong, rich paint color for the walls – since the room is not in constant use, you can afford to be more adventurous; and deep tones provide a dramatic backdrop for special occasions, setting off pictures and mirrors well. Crimson was a popular color in Victorian times, but terra-cotta or salmon may be easier on the eye. Forest green and deep blue are favored alternatives. If you prefer wallpaper, look for classical stripes, damask patterns or Oriental designs of vines or trellis. Crisp white paintwork picks out detailed moldings, or use a different tone of the same color in shiny gloss.

Strong colors make a good background for gilt-framed pictures, sparkling mirrors and wall-mounted candelabra. For a paler scheme, choose luxurious creams or buttery shades, with imposing patterns on walls or curtains to create a grand flourish.

Striped wallpaper teamed with a distinctive archive print in the recess, provides an elegant background for formal furnishings. A pale ceiling adds a sense of height.
Rose chintz curtains add muted warmth, complementing the rich luster of the polished wood and Oriental rug.
Matching glass-fronted display cabinets add to the graceful symmetry of the formal setting.
Wall plaques, mirrors and traditional china strike an unmistakably Classic note.

STYLE POINTERS

 WALLS Strong/deep: plain rich colors in matte or gloss finish; paint effects – marbling, colorwashing or classical stenciled motifs.
Wallpapers: stripes, scrolling damask-style patterns or Chinese influences – wisteria, trellis or bamboo designs.

 WINDOWS Curtains: heavily swagged drapes, rosettes and tassels; gilt, brass or dark wood poles.
Blinds: heavily trimmed Austrian or London blinds, or Roman blinds framed by decorative valances.

 FLOORING Traditional: wall-to-wall carpet, plain or with scrolling, small motifs or a border; polished wood floor.
Rugs: richly colored Turkish or Oriental-style rug, positioned centrally under the table.

 FABRICS Rich: damask, velvet or silk; traditional large-scale patterned chintzes or linens; tapestry, needlepoint or woven patterns for upholstery.

 FURNITURE Period: mahogany, satinwood, rosewood or cherry.
Table and chairs: ideally, a matching set – upholstered, armless chairs with wooden frames; circular, oval or rectangular table; carved sideboard or reproduction glass-fronted cabinet.

 LIGHTING Elaborate: grand crystal or gilt central candelabra fixture, plus discreet side lighting; wall sconces or shaded lamps; dimmer switches; silver candlesticks or candelabra.

 ACCESSORIES Refined: oil paintings in wood or gilded frames; antique-style mirrors; delicate china; crystal decanters and flower vases, silver serving dishes; white linen or damask tablecloth/napkins.

➤ *Less traditional but strong on impact, warm mulberry red brings the walls closer for a cozy feel in this clever scheme. Below dado level, a cool cream gives a lighter touch, in harmony with the blue stain and airy flower print of the chairs. Wrought-iron light fixtures add a dramatic line.*

CLASSIC STYLE FURNISHINGS

The dining table is the focal point of the room, and should be centrally placed, with enough surrounding space for chairs to be drawn back easily. A glossy polished wood table, with drop leaves or add-in sections to accommodate larger parties, is ideal. Surround it with delicate, wooden-framed chairs, which may be upholstered.

Built-in cabinets and shelving have decorative molding; alternatively, set a period sideboard along one wall for storage. A marble-topped side table, or a low chest of drawers, is a useful set-down point for dishes. A glass-fronted cabinet can display crystal and porcelain.

One or two large pictures, framed in dark wood or gilt, can be lit with special picture lights or spots for added atmosphere. Choose old-fashioned portraits, animal pictures or landscapes in rich colors, or perhaps flower and plant engravings for a lighter scheme. Alternatively, mount large decorative plates or a framed collection of family photographs on the wall.

Make a dramatic gesture at the window with elaborately embellished curtains in sumptuous fabrics. Dining rooms are more often used in the evening so you need not be so concerned about blocking out natural light. Elegant swags and tails, with rich trim-mings, create a luxurious air of comfort, but simple full curtains on a heavy, decorative pole can be just as impressive. Hang chunky tassels from the ends for added grandeur. For a smaller room, opt for a blind dressed up with a striking scarf drape or valance.

Lighting is important for atmosphere. A central candelabra fixture should have low-wattage bulbs; use flickering candle-type bulbs or a dimmer switch so it does not dazzle. Place one or two small candle lamps symmetrically on the mantel shelf or on small tables, then create an intimate glow on the table with candles in silver candlesticks.

Set the table with a snowy damask or linen cloth; placemats with gilt edging are practical and formal. Tableware should be china or porcelain, pretty and delicate or plain and elegant. Look for silver servers, salt and pepper shakers and other decorative items at antique stores or garage sales. Silver-plated or steel cutlery should be as elegant as possible, preferably of a period design.

Finally, dress up the room and table with fresh flowers. Low arrangements, or wispy trails of flowers and leaves around a candelabra, make a perfect centerpiece.

▶ *Soft white linens and twirling white candles can't fail to impress – it's a classic formula that complements fine china and sparkling glassware.*

▶ *Moody blue striped wallpaper makes a subtle background for a traditional gilt-framed fish-eye mirror, topped with its own gilded wreath. Wooden picture frames and silver serving jugs are all important elements of the Classic dining room.*

▼ *Finely tapered legs and delicate carving characterize these pretty chairs, which would suit a light, airy room.*

Simple is often the best: choose a graceful silver container and pack it with vibrant blooms for a splash of color.

Shiny scarlet chintz in a classic Oriental print is the perfect partner for lacquered red walls. The elaborate drapery is boldly lined in black to frame the window theatrically.

Look out for old crystal decanters, to hold fine port or liqueurs. They don't need to be a matching set – each one has its own individual charm.

STYLE DETAILS

Time spent on decorative touches in a dining room are well worth the effort – details can be appreciated at leisure by your guests as they enjoy a lengthy meal. Cleverly folded napkins, sparkling crystal and fragrant fresh flowers all add to the sense of occasion, and are an eloquent expression of the art of hospitality. Make time to prepare the table before a dinner or celebration, and look for individual, unusual touches that may provide talking points for guests.

Smartly folded napkins always give a flourish to a place setting. This elegant method of folding finishes with two tails of neatly splaying pleats.

A low, symmetrical flower arrangement is ideal for a formal dinner party. Include a few highly scented flowers for romantic wafts of perfume across the table.

This floor-length tablecloth with its bullion fringe provides a luxurious solution to the problem of hiding a less than glamorous dining table.

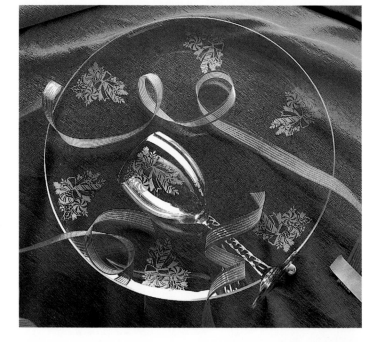

Hand-etched glass has a delicate, exclusive appeal all its own. Purchase press-on decals and apply them to your own pieces, so you can create unique imitations of this age-old craft from a plain piece of glass.

AMERICAN COUNTRY DINING ROOM

*The American Country dining room is homey and
inviting – the style is basically functional, yet the furnishings
and accessories give it a delightful period charm.*

Painted woodwork, in a darker shade than the walls, is a hallmark of American Country style. An heirloom-style table and chairs in glowing wood, simple furnishings and charming handcrafted accessories are also typical of this relaxed, understated look. Primitive folk paintings (inset) – portraits, landscapes or studies of animals and plants – make a typical wall display.

The nostalgic American Country style is very much a practical choice for today's informal dining room. It combines simplicity and function with a cozy, 'lived-in' look, but without the clutter. The American Country dining room has always had the family and friends in mind. Its understated streamlining means hearty meals are served and cleared away with ease, while an air of comfort offers encouragement to stay on, chatting round the table.

American Country style has grown from an eclectic blend of traditional European styles that were brought to North America by the early settlers. The legacy of a simple way of life, using treasured belongings and locally made rustic pieces, together with a rich heritage of handicrafts, is apparent in the various elements that make up its charming, folk-inspired look.

CREATING THE STYLE

Plain walls, strong yet muted color for woodwork and painted furniture, and simple homespun-style fabrics capture the essence of the American Country style. Easily the greatest influence on the American Country dining room has come from the Shakers – a small religious sect who believed that beauty was in simplicity, materials and craftsmanship. Their enduring design ideas are seen in the elegant, clean lines of sideboards, tables, chairs and distinctive peg rails – designed to hold hanging cupboards, shelves, chairs and utensils – through to the smallest metal candleholder, and steamed-wood storage boxes and trays.

Combined with the Shaker influence is the so-called Pennsylvania Dutch style – a mixture of German and Scandinavian craft styles, epitomized by pretty folk patterns incorporating hearts, birds and flowers. Traditionally painted or stenciled on walls to imitate wallpaper, they are also worked on furniture, floors and tinware, and as patchwork and appliqué motifs.

STYLE POINTERS

 WALLS Plain/pale: smooth, traditional cream or off-white paint; American Country colors; colorwash; stencil patterns.

 WOODWORK Muted color/sheen: satin finish or eggshell; typical American Country color palette: cranberry, turkey/barn red, mustard, nutmeg, blue-tinged forest green, muted gray-green, gray-blue.
Wood paneling: natural polished wood dado and peg rails.

 WINDOWS Uncluttered: traditional sash windows with wooden shutters/slatted wood blinds; simple curtain styles.

 FABRICS Homespun: natural cotton for curtains and tablecloths – gingham and checks, calico prints/stencil designs; patchwork.

 FLOORING Plain/neutral: polished hardwood; painted and stenciled boards; neutral carpet; plain tiles.
Rugs: hooked or braided rag rugs; painted/stenciled canvas floor cloth; sisal matting.

 FURNITURE Simple/rustic: inspired by Shaker designs – freestanding, clean lines in maple and cherry wood or pine or beech; wooden sideboard and hanging cupboards – painted/stenciled; decorated with punched tin panels.
Table and chairs: period styles; polished trestle/drop-leaf table; ladder or spindle-back chairs; wood, rush or upholstered seats; stripped farmhouse styles.

 LIGHTING Period/wrought iron: pendant candle-style candelabra fixture; matching wall sconces; glass/oil table lamps; Shaker-style candleholder; beeswax candles.

 ACCESSORIES Period charm: shelves; wooden bowls; oval stacking boxes; trays; primitive folk paintings; salt-glaze pottery; mainly white period-style china dinner service, bone-effect handles on cutlery; chunky stemware.

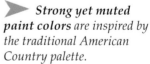

The traditional vegetable pigment colors used in American Country decorations have a subtle, muted glow. In a modern interpretation, these stripes capture the period colors well. The simple iron candle fixture, Country dining chairs and scrubbed table add period charm without following the style too rigidly.

Strong yet muted paint colors are inspired by the traditional American Country palette.
Stained and polished floorboards and a sisal mat create a rustic look.
Country check fabric for the window blind has a cheerful, homespun look.
Clean-lined furniture – the table, chairs and dresser are all influenced by the simplicity of American Country style.
Accessories in wood and earthenware are both decorative and functional.

COUNTRY FURNISHINGS

Ideally, the dining table and chairs in the American Country dining room should be a period, antique style in dark wood or fruitwood. Alternatively, a simple Shaker-inspired trestle or drop-leaf table and ladder- or spindle-back chairs is very much the style. You can capture the look with a pine farmhouse table and chairs, and paint the chairs and the legs of the table in an American Country color.

In keeping with a traditional, simple lifestyle, the fabrics and furnishings in the American Country dining room are comfortable but unpretentious. Window treatments are functional – shutters or slatted wood blinds in American Country colors, or fabric blinds and curtain styles with cased or softly gathered headings. Ginghams and checks, sprigged cotton and calico prints or, for a more modern interpretation, denim or chambray would be fabric choices. Tablecloths and linens are also simple; an heirloom-style starched white damask or cutwork cloth and napkins is appropriate for formal dining; otherwise gingham or cotton check tablecloth or placemats, perhaps decorated with stenciled or appliquéd motifs, are typical of the style.

Cover chair seat pads to match curtain fabrics, or make a feature with patchwork or needlework sampler cushions. Under the dining table, a handmade braided or hooked fabric strip rug would add an authentic touch. Alternatively, you could make a traditional painted or stenciled canvas floor cloth.

➤ *This elegant dining room with its solid, dark wood table and ladder-back chairs, graceful wrought-iron candelabra and pretty calico blinds, captures the simplicity of the American Country look without slavishly adopting the more rustic elements of the style.*

◄ *A collection of antique kitchen paraphernalia makes a nostalgic wall display. The American Country theme is accented by the corn and muffin tins and the framed fruit poster.*

▲ Muted cranberry red is a typical American Country color. Here it is an integral part of a coordinated color scheme that moves easily from the kitchen to the dining room. Country details include the stamp print checks, the calico tablecloth and the black iron door and drawer handles.

➤ A painted sideboard is an important American Country style feature. In typical muted blue, this piece is weathered to enhance a rustic nautical theme, and accessorized with witty period details.

STYLE DETAILS

Shaker-style accessories – trays and boxes made from steamed wood – are typical of the American Country style. Use them to store cutlery – bone-effect handles are authentic – and table linen, or just put them on display.

Metal details based on traditional forged designs add impact and period style. Look for curve-ended curtain poles, heart-shaped hooks, cupboard and drawer handles, graceful candelabra and wall sconces. Punched tin panels on a cupboard front and freestanding metal silhouette designs pick up the folksy influence. Other touches include beeswax candles, vine garlands and fresh Country-style flower displays.

▶ *The folk-art influence of Pennsylvania Dutch designs is shown in these pretty punched tin door panels. You can create the same effect on any paneled door.*

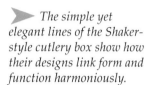

▶ *The simple yet elegant lines of the Shaker-style cutlery box show how their designs link form and function harmoniously.*

◀ *In this lovingly created dining room, authentic American Country touches include stenciled walls, a peg rail, hanging baskets, a homespun check window swag and the forged iron fittings, candelabra and animal silhouette. Well-worn polished wood and heirloom pieces complete the period look.*

▲ *Colors can epitomize a style, and barn red and gray-blue are typically American Country. Use them in your dining room for a peg and dado rail and a painted chair; then add a heart wreath as a rustic detail.*

Soft Contemporary Living Room

*The hallmarks of Soft Contemporary style are comfort
and practicality, achieved by combining traditional and modern
influences to create an informal, uncluttered look.*

First impressions of a Soft Contemporary living room should be of a pleasing, light and airy room where traditional and modern influences combine stylishly in a relaxed, harmonious way. Comfortable furniture is complemented by unfussy furnishings in quality fabrics and fashionable color blends. Even when your room is small, you can create this well-ordered look by choosing a pale, fresh color scheme, good lighting, and small-scale patterns and furniture.

*A light-enhancing color
scheme, comfortable furniture,
fresh fabrics and up-to-date styling
details, such as the twisted metal
candlestick, the framed screen prints
and the tie-topped curtains, all combine
to give this Soft Contemporary living
room its orderly appeal.*

*Practical accessories such as
these customized curtain holdbacks
are typical of the simple extras that
make this style so attractive.*

CREATING THE STYLE

Contemporary styles are versatile – they work well in modern or period homes and are equally practical for singles who want a flexible style with a degree of portability, and for growing families, where smart but functional furniture and adaptable decorations are primary considerations.

To achieve the Soft Contemporary look, use a low-key, fairly neutral background. Aim to create a subtle tonal link between walls, ceiling and floor. Avoid strong color contrasts between walls and floor as these visually 'break up' the area and counter the spacious effect.

Opt for pale walls, perhaps with a dado in a marginally deeper shade to blend with the flooring; and choose simple, light-toned storage units and occasional tables to promote the feeling of light and space. This approach allows plenty of leeway for you to introduce stronger color accents in the soft furnishings and accessories, and to add brightly colored rugs, pillows, pictures and flowers – the details that give the room its individual look.

STYLE POINTERS

 WALLS Pale/neutral: plain shades. Paint effects such as sponging or colorwashing can be used to add subtle decorative touches.
Wallpapers: self-colored pattern motifs or subtle stripes. Coordinating borders and dados complement the effect.

 WINDOWS Curtains: informal variations of traditional styles; full-length curtains with simple gathered or tab headings; soft cornices and relaxed swags; wood or metal curtain poles; fabric or metal tiebacks or cords.
Blinds: softly structured fabric blinds such as Roman and pleated blinds; wooden slatted and venetian blinds or plantation shutters.

 FLOORING Pale/neutral: plain, wall-to-wall carpet; natural fiber matting; stripped boards; wood blocks and rugs.

 FABRICS Unfussy: pale/neutral slubb silks; woven checks and stripes; stylized florals. Solid-color accents.

 FURNITURE Informal but streamlined: blond or limed wood; light-colored wicker; glass with dark metal frames. Compact storage.
Seating: comfortable and practical; traditionally upholstered sofas and chairs – can be unmatched in mixed colors or matched in neutrals, solids, checks and stripes, or discreet self-color prints.

 LIGHTING Diffused: sconces, torchères and table lamps harmonize with the color scheme and cast a gentle glow.

 ACCESSORIES Informal: casual throws; simple pillows with stylish details; light wood picture frames and containers; wicker baskets; ironwork candlesticks; simple flower arrangements and specimen plants add dramatic interest.

▲ *Plain white walls and neutral details* provide a versatile background for simple furnishings and stylish accessories.

The informal window treatment shows how a relaxed version of traditional swags and tails elegantly complements a simple slatted blind.

Natural fiber floorcovering blends with the neutral walls, helping to create a spacious look. The rug provides color and pattern interest.

Comfortable seating in neutral colors is enlivened by color accent pillows.

Clean-lined occasional tables in pale wood and metal flatter the simple lines and color of the seating and accessories.

In this version of the Soft Contemporary look, discreetly patterned wallcovering and natural flooring provide a neutral backdrop for the light, streamlined furniture and smartly striped sofas. With fresh flower focal points and toning color accents, the effect is one of airy, uncluttered comfort.

Hazy yellows harmonize with natural light to create a wonderfully restful atmosphere. An informally draped curtain swag adds a bravura touch of color while lush house plants enhance the fresh, natural feel.

▼ Ice cream-colored gerbera daisies can add a bright splash of color in a Soft Contemporary living room. Fresh flowers are an inexpensive way to experiment with new color schemes or accent colors before embarking on a complete decorative face-lift.

SOFT CONTEMPORARY FURNISHINGS

Classically shaped sofas and chairs are key pieces in the Soft Contemporary living room. They may be unmatched, or comfortably worn, but their friendly presence is part of the style. If you have neutral upholstery, give it a color or texture boost with throws and pillows; combine matte and silky fabrics, and solids with stripes, checks or prints.

Alternatively, choose a patterned cover fabric and color-matched solids to link the differently shaped pieces, and team these with pillows in toning or contrasting solids or coordinated prints.

To accentuate the light, airy feel, choose curtains or fabric blinds to tone with the walls. You can do this with neutral solids, or patterned fabrics with a toning, pale background. Generously draped, full-length curtains add to the comfort factor; catch them back with decorative holdbacks or knotted cords and ties. Alternatively, accentuate striking window shapes with simple blinds or improvised swags.

Lighting also plays an important part – the fresh daytime look needs to be complemented in the evening with soft, targeted pools of light. Use discreet wall sconces – uplights painted to match the walls to illuminate the general area – then add stylish table lamps to serve the seating areas. Soft Contemporary styles include bold but simply styled vase lamps and shades or pared-down contemporary wood and metal designs.

▼ An informal grouping of pictures and objets in warm-toned natural materials epitomizes the Soft Contemporary approach to room style. Here, the wooden mantel shelf provides the ideal base for this pretty display.

Paying special attention to the accessories in a Soft Contemporary living room makes all the difference to its character. Here, a few carefully selected items – metalwork lamp fixtures, fresh flowers in bright contrast colors and a framed display of unusual plant seeds add a stamp of individuality to this Soft Contemporary living room.

Natural materials and the handcrafted look are all in keeping with Soft Contemporary look. Pale wicker furniture and plump cushions in strong accent colors, a modern light wood occasional table with metal legs and soft-toned lighting all ensure a comfortable, welcoming feel.

A traditional sofa, covered in bold checks, provides the modern twist that's typical of the Soft Contemporary style. Contrasted and coordinated pillows and an informal wicker table add lively color and texture accents.

STYLE DETAILS

Style details – those finishing touches that allow you to stamp your personality on a scheme with accessories and color accents – are essential additions to any home.

On this page a variety of accessories and ideas will be featured. Below are some suggestions for adding individual touches to a Soft Contemporary living room.

▲ *Glass-topped table* This interesting table fits well in a Soft Contemporary room, and sometimes can even be adapted, as here, to become a showcase for favorite collectibles.

▲ *Miniature dried moss topiaries* Create unusual space fillers with these mini topiaries. They look charming grouped with other accessories on a shelf or table, or used alone to add a hint of natural color.

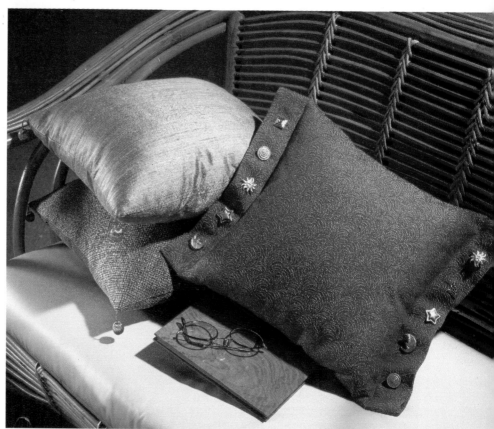

▶ *Gilt trims and tassels* Attention to detail always pays dividends; adding gilt button trims and shiny ball tassels to these simple pillows gives them a stylish twist and creates a visual link with other metal accents in the room.

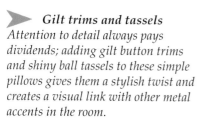

COUNTRY COTTAGE LIVING ROOM

*Capture the enduring charm of a country cottage with
a light-enhancing color scheme, bright and cozy furnishings,
pretty fabrics and, of course, country garden flowers.*

A Country Cottage-style living room is essentially a comfortable, cozy place – a warm and friendly room that is a welcome retreat from the hectic pace of city life. Fortunately, you do not have to live in a period home with beams or inglenooks to capture the essence of cottage style, which has more to do with creating an ambience with color, furnishings and accessories than with any particular period or authentic architectural details.

Since country cottages come in many guises, from old vacation homes and guest houses to lower-level conversions and suburban bungalows, there are no hard-and-fast styling rules. However, the decorative threads that run through all cottage-style variations share a freshness and charm.

Nothing in the cottage sitting room should look obviously brand-new – the style is about integrating an eclectic mix of old and new, placing simple, well-loved period pieces alongside newer additions. Whether you favor nostalgic, old-fashioned schemes, chic and minimalist rustic looks, or just prefer pretty country-style florals and handcrafted details, simplicity, practicality and comfort are constant themes.

A pale color scheme creates a feeling of light and space, while period-style furniture and splashes of glowing color in comfortable soft furnishings add warmth in this essentially cozy room. Handcrafted details such as fragrant potpourri fruits (below) are typical Country Cottage accessories.

43

CREATING THE STYLE

Low ceilings and small windows are typical features in cottage living rooms, so making the most of natural light is often an important consideration – as it is in many modern homes. In modestly sized rooms, create an illusion of brightness and space with pale painted walls – either lined, or rough-cast plaster – and pastel tints, soft whites and creams, and with subtle paint effects such as colorwashing and sponging. Alternatively, choose a light-colored wallcovering with a discreet sprig print. To create a cozier effect in larger rooms, color the walls with warm mid-tones – spice colors, coral pink and terra-cotta; or choose larger, subtle florals, balanced with cooler accents such as fresh green or old gold. A dado or patterned wallcovering border at dado rail level also helps to suggest Country Cottage proportions.

Create a mellow look underfoot with polished or stained boards and rugs or alternatively, choose a faux flagstone-effect floorcovering. Cover with a large, slightly color-faded Oriental or traditional wool rug, or a quieter plain sisal or cotton mat for the central area. Otherwise, lay a plain, neutral wall-to-wall carpet and small rugs.

A period-style, cast-iron fireplace with a pine or painted wood surround, traditional screen and accessories, or an open brick hearth with a fire basket will create an unbeatable focal point. Modern 'real flame' effect fires can add an authentic touch without the hard work of a real fire.

STYLE POINTERS

 WALLS Plain/discreet pattern: smooth or rough-cast plaster; pale and mid-tone paint, wallcovering with subtle, small-scale motifs; coordinating or floral borders; stenciled motifs; paneled dado; picture or dado rail.

 WINDOWS Curtains: simple gathered/tab heading styles, lined and unlined on metal rods/wood poles; frilled valance headings; informal fabric-covered cornices/draped poles; café-style sheers; old-fashioned wooden shutters.
Blinds: roller and Austrian styles.

 FABRICS Florals/plains: cotton and chintz florals and fruits, sprigs, checks, stripes; linen/ticking; soft woolens; velvets; canvaswork; lace/embroidery.

 FLOORING Polished boards/rugs: limed, stained, polished or painted boards; neutral wall-to-wall carpet; sisal flooring; faux stone; traditional/Oriental wool, canvaswork or cotton rugs.

 FURNITURE Period-style/comfortable: distressed dark wood or pine; simple, traditional upholstery for chairs/sofa, loose/slipcovers; antique occasional/folding tables; painted, crackle-glazed chests and wall cupboards with stencil or decoupage decorations; TV/music equipment in pine/wooden housing; alcove shelves and cupboards.

 LIGHTING: Traditional/cozy: central glass bowl/lantern or simple wood/wrought-iron candelabra; candle lamp wall sconces; wood/wrought-iron wall lights with tailored/gathered floral or plain fabric shades; candlestick/vase base table lamps with plain/floral fabric shades; brass/wrought-iron/wood standard lamps.

 ACCESSORIES: Heirloom/rustic: traditional fireplace furniture; distressed/dark wood, pine or gilt picture/mirror frames; old prints, botanical studies; period-style china; small boxes; mantel/wall clock; plants in cachepots; ruffled/buttoned cushions; wool rugs and throws; cottage garden/dried/silk flowers.

A warm and cozy color scheme creates a welcoming Country Cottage atmosphere in a modern home.

Slipcovers for sofas and chairs in attractive cotton checks and stripes are practical and informal.

Pretty floral fabrics have a simple Country freshness.

Natural wood flooring and a modest cotton rug are typical Country-style features.

A period-style fireplace and accessories enhance the feeling for traditional comforts.

The quiet charms of a well-appointed, traditional Country Cottage parlor are evident here. The comfortable setting is enhanced by the warm glow of the table lamps, which cast a flattering light on furniture and furnishings, and the pretty china and collectibles.

LIVING ROOM FURNISHINGS

Sitting comfortably is a priority in every cottage-style living room. Generously proportioned, traditionally upholstered sofas and chairs with a desirable 'lived-in' look, are totally at one with their surroundings. Under fresh cotton or linen slipcovers – in cheerful solids, florals, checks or stripes – their fillings may have sagged a little, but this is all part of relaxed, Country charm. Plumped pillows with simple cotton, needlepoint, embroidererd or patchwork covers, and bright wool blankets and throws are added for extra comfort.

If modern gadgetry, in the form of television and music equipment, intrudes too obviously into your Country Cottage idyll, house it in custom-made cupboards. These are available in rustic pine, or you can convert an existing piece of furniture such as a dresser or alcove cupboard for the purpose. There are also special tables with a hidden TV shelf, which you can dress with fabric to match your upholstered pieces or curtains.

The curtain treatments depend on the window size, but all should pull back far enough to let in plenty of light. Cotton and chintz curtains in simple gathered or tab-head styles on poles or rods are typical, although thicker fabrics such as linen and velvets may have pleated headings or covered cornices. Matching tiebacks or cords are appropriate.

▶ *Succulent summer fruits have an enduring appeal as fabric prints, and here they highlight the Country Cottage theme. Teamed with simple brick walls painted pastel green, warm wood tones, crisp white and rich, verdant green, the effect is cozy and inviting.*

▲ *A design of full-blown roses frames the French door, and creates a pretty background for the traditional sofa. This is dressed in an understated floral print, and accessorized with a collection of ruffled pillows. Again, pink and green create a favorite Country-style color scheme.*

▶ *As an essentially Country-style flower, flamboyant foxgloves will be a constant reminder of country walks and cottage gardens. They create a dramatic focal point in this setting, where rustic simplicity and cozy comforts say "less is more."*

▲ A restful, summertime atmosphere is created by the charming pink and green color scheme. This is offset by warm white walls, floral print curtains, and an abundance of fresh flowering geraniums.

➤ A fresh and bright color scheme, romantic floral-print curtains and a pretty tabletop arrangement form an integral part of the cottage look.

STYLE DETAILS

One of the attractions of Country Cottage style is the way old and new elements blend together naturally. You can mix antique collectibles with modern pieces – not just with furniture and soft furnishings, but with accessories, too.

Old, starched lace tablecloths look just as pretty on a small table with a modern china tea set as with antique porcelain. Use them, too, for tabletop arrangements, where period silver frames sit alongside modern, wooden or ceramic frames and small *objets*. Illuminate your display with a pretty table lamp – choose a candlestick design, ginger jar or rustic earthenware base shape.

Plants and flowers probably have the biggest impact as Country-style accessories. Aim to have a large vase or jug filled generously with seasonal flowers – either fresh or silk, or a mixture of both. On the windowsill, arrange pots of flowers and house plants, such as geraniums, scented jasmine and violets, or pretty miniature topiaries.

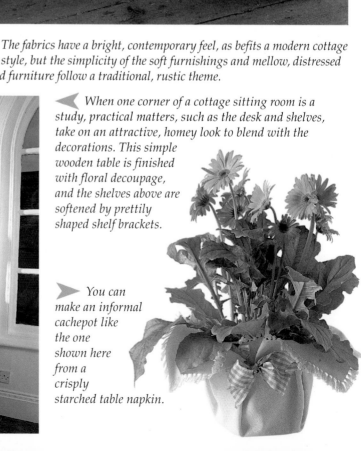

The fabrics have a bright, contemporary feel, as befits a modern cottage style, but the simplicity of the soft furnishings and mellow, distressed wood furniture follow a traditional, rustic theme.

Every element here epitomizes Old-World charm, from the dark wood cottage chairs and chest that frame the window, to the weathered beam, mini-print curtains and pretty flowering plants on the windowsill.

When one corner of a cottage sitting room is a study, practical matters, such as the desk and shelves, take on an attractive, homey look to blend with the decorations. This simple wooden table is finished with floral decoupage, and the shelves above are softened by prettily shaped shelf brackets.

You can make an informal cachepot like the one shown here from a crisply starched table napkin.

48

SCANDINAVIAN LIVING ROOM

*Calm and elegant, Scandinavian style creates a living area imbued
with the grace of former years, but the pale, restrained furnishings
have a fresh, airy feel in tune with a modern Country look.*

Pale wooden floors, simple checked fabrics and delicate colors are the hallmarks of the enduring and versatile Scandinavian look. This Country style works to maximize the watery sun in Northern European countries such as Sweden and Norway, which have to make the most of their precious daylight hours; but it has increasingly become a popular look for modern homes. Used in a living room, it's an ideal way to create a soothing yet elegant place where you can relax or entertain.

Scandinavian style traditionally ranges from the rustic look of country homes, with simple wooden settles, rag runners and beaten tin artifacts, to the graceful carved or

Cool gray-green woodwork and stenciling is set against sunny straw-colored walls in an elegant and restrained Scandinavian scheme. An elaborate chair and gilt candlestick sconces make a typical contrast with the simple cotton blind and painted wooden settle.

painted furniture, chandeliers and fine porcelain of grander Gustavian homes – the term 'Gustavian' refers to Gustav III, king of Sweden in the eighteenth century.

Bare floors and clear, pale walls reflect the light around the room. Windows are left unadorned or are dressed with lightweight, unlined fabrics, to flood the room with as much light as possible.

CREATING THE STYLE

Painted surfaces are a strong element of Scandinavian style. The palette is soft, with muted colors that are restful on the eye: baby blue, watery turquoise and silver gray, together with pale neutrals such as cream, off-white and stone. Other typical shades are gray-green and a muddy peachy pink, or pale straw.

Use flat paints on walls for a dull, chalky finish, and eggshell or satin paint for woodwork. You can use subtle paint effects – colorwashing, soft ragging and glazing – to highlight any features, or add a simple stenciled border of hearts and spiraling leaves for interest. Period features such as beaded paneling and ceiling roses evoke the grander Gustavian style, while tongue-and-groove boarding to dado level is more rustic. Fireplaces should be wood with blue-and-white tiled insets, or plain marble; a freestanding stove adds an authentic touch.

Wallcoverings and borders that suit the look are readily available: small sprigs on a pale background, simple stripes, or motifs such as windmills and clogs, taken from Delft tiles, are all in keeping.

The Scandinavian style floor is bare wood – boards or parquet. You can sand and paint existing floorboards, but if possible lighten them with lime or bleach them before sealing.

STYLE POINTERS

 WALLS Soft/muted: subtle blues, greens and grays with white or cream; dragged woodwork; stenciled borders of sprigs and hearts.
Wallcovering: simple stripes, trellis, sprigs and stylized florals; imitation Delft tile effects.

 WINDOWS Curtains: light, unlined fabrics tied or gathered on a simple, painted wood or iron pole; Italian strung style on gilt pole; wispy loops of muslin.
Blinds: wooden shutters or venetians, Roman, London, roller or tie-up blinds.

 FLOORING Pale/hard: strip or parquet wooden floorboards in light tones, or limed/painted; natural coir or jute floorcoverings.
Rugs: flat-weave, folk-style rugs; striped cotton mats, rag rugs, cross-stitch or Aubusson-style tapestry mats.

 FABRICS Light/cool: cottons and linens in blue or red checks, stripes and simple folk designs; plain calico, flocked voile, muslin; some needlepoint and tapestry on chairs and cushions; cross-stitch embroidery.

 FURNITURE Painted/carved wood: period pieces with distressed paint effects and/or stenciled; plain wood with cutout details; cupboards with wooden, glass or chicken-wire doors; simple upright sofas with wooden legs and arms; wooden settles with narrow box cushions; lightly upholstered period sofas and chairs; slipcovers and seat covers.

 LIGHTING Period: painted wood, gilt and glass, or iron chandelier; wall sconces in tin, gilt or iron with tiny checked candle shades; porcelain table lamps with paper shades; candle/oil lanterns and simple candlesticks.

 ACCESSORIES Period/rustic: blue-and-white china and lamp bases; dried flower or twig wreaths; oval wooden boxes and wire baskets; period sculptures; delicate fluted glass.

Subtle gray walls and off-white paintwork provide a cool, restrained backdrop.
Blue-and-white fabrics and china give a crisp, airy Scandinavian look.
A wood-framed sofa is softened with a simple box cushion and bolsters.
Lightly upholstered chairs and an ottoman display refined detailing.
Period-style lighting adds elegant Scandinavian style detail.

A bold red-and-white check is offset by soft yellow paintwork for an unusual but authentic Scandinavian scheme. The fabric lines the walls and appears again at the window, surrounding the neatly slipcovered sofa and imposing chandelier with a warm glow.

SCANDINAVIAN FURNISHINGS

The Scandinavian style room has an airy, sparsely furnished look; push furniture back to walls to create an expanse of bare floor. In place of a squashy sofa, make tailored box cushions for a wooden settle or even a painted garden bench with neat bolsters at each end. Modern seating with simple, clean lines and tapered legs blends well with the look; or seek out elegant period sofas and chairs with wooden or open arms, spindly legs and graceful curves. Upholstery has a homespun look – solid linens and cottons, checks, stripes, or toile de Jouy prints, with pastoral scenes.

Built-in or freestanding painted wood cupboards act as storage space for hi-fi equipment and books, and can have glass or wire panels to display classic blue-and-white china.

Occasional pieces such as side tables or coffee tables are kept to a minimum. A butler's tray makes a useful and versatile addition: hang the base on pegs on the wall when not in use, to make for more space. Simple painted wood tables or chests for lamps and accessories should be placed against the wall.

Windows are left as bare as possible to maximize light. Curtains, if any, are unlined, and simply hung on wood or iron poles, or perhaps topped with a narrow serpentine cornice in wood or fabric. A narrow valance of gingham,

▶ *Cover a sofa in a slipcover of washable cotton checked fabric to give it the freshly laundered Scandinavian look. The faded coral and ochre of the pillows makes a warm alternative to cool blues and greens.*

▼ *Almost every surface in this living room has a coat of subtle blue-gray paint; details such as beaded panels, the lyre-shaped table and patterned fabrics add interest and life to the scheme.*

▲ *Crisp turquoise stripes and checks, and rustic, pale cream paneled walls make a precise background for the exuberantly flowing curves of the sofa and the delicate tracery of a wirework candleholder.*

◄ *Neat details on soft furnishings are a hallmark of the Scandinavian look. Cushions are finished with contrast buttons and borders, while the slipcover on a chair has tiny split corners.*

muslin or cutwork, or a wispy voile drape, is sometimes the only window treatment; or it is combined with shutters or a blind.

Lighting makes a distinct period statement. A central chandelier can be wood, iron or a grander version in gilt with simple glass droplets for elegance; or opt for pierced tin wall sconces to imitate candlelight, for a more rustic look. Look for styles backed with small mirrors for extra gleam; tiny candle bulbs can be left bare, or covered with plain parchment or gingham shades. Pierced or pleated paper shades top simple wooden or china lamp bases. Candles in storm glasses, or tiny nightlights, create a pretty glow.

Soften the bare wood floor with one or two rugs – a simple striped cotton mat for a countrified room, or a pretty Aubusson style in pale colors if you are aiming for a more elegant effect.

53

STYLE DETAILS

Keep accessories to a well-chosen minimum to avoid a cluttered look. A plain wood or gilt-framed mirror increases light and elegance; one or two period engravings in black frames, botanical prints or small silhouettes hung with a checked picture ribbon grace the walls. A plaster figurine or bust, or pretty glass and china, are typical of Gustavian elegance.

For a more homey look, hang a willow or dried flower and herb wreath on the wall; pierced tin figurines, candle boxes and shelf units have the same rustic style, together with the oval wooden boxes made famous by the American Shaker settlers. Tiny red bows tied on candle sconces, or topping curtains, add a pretty, homey touch.

◄ *Look for reproduction chairs such as this. Its graceful lines and delicate carved details are given understated elegance by a coat of dove gray paint.*

► *Folk artifacts such as this charming simple embroidery, in its subtle blues, have just the right look, mounted in a blond wood frame.*

◄ *Simple cotton runners and rag rugs are in keeping with unimposing Scandinavian style, and add a little softness underfoot.*

▲ *The tidy symmetry of closely grouped furniture against the wall has a restful air of order and calm. It leaves empty stretches of floor to create an impression of space.*

DRAMATIC LIVING ROOM

Creating a visual impact underlines the decorative approach
in the Dramatic living room, where mood and ambience, glorious color,
and a taste for the theatrical are the starting points.

When you decorate a living room in Dramatic style, your flamboyant statement is sure to impress – whether in a subtle way, with an exquisitely balanced composition of light, form and color, or through the full "curtains up" impact of an overtly theatrical or glamorous theme.

Choosing the living room as a focus for daring decorating tastes is particularly rewarding for outgoing personalities, as in this setting your imaginative efforts are sure to be noticed. If you are an extrovert, or you simply want to try something different, you can follow an avant-garde,

Imperial purple creates a spectacular backdrop for some dramatically different furniture and furnishings. Lashings of gold – a Dramatic style favorite – highlight the extravagant look, which could also be complemented by an exuberantly jewel-trimmed chandelier (left).

romantic or escapist theme, or celebrate color, pattern and style in an exciting and uninhibited way. Decorating your living room under the Dramatic banner will reveal your adventurous personality, as well as a highly developed imagination and sense of fun.

CREATING THE STYLE

Arguably the first and most important consideration for creating a Dramatic style living room is color. You can never underestimate its power, and it really does offer the quickest and least expensive way to create an impact or suggest an atmosphere. A bold, richly glowing color scheme is an obvious starting point for dramatic effect, but a breathtakingly delicate or all-white color scheme can have just as powerful an effect in the appropriate setting.

You probably have an idea of the kind of effect you would like to create – color preferences, mood and furnishing style. With your theme in mind, the next step is to plan a focal point in the room. This may be an existing feature such as a striking window or impressive fireplace, or you may want to create the impression that these desirable features already exist. This is where the fantasy element of Dramatic style comes into play – just as set designers can transform a stage, you can use fabric and paint to turn the frankly mundane into something special.

Lighting also plays an important part in this transformation. Apart from choosing an eye-catching main light fixture, a dimmer switch, discreetly placed sconces, torchères and spots are prerequisites for creating atmosphere and for highlighting key features.

STYLE POINTERS

 WALLS Rich/flamboyant: brilliant, bold color; color glazes; faux paint effects – stone, verdigris, marble; murals; trompe l'oeil; classical motifs and moldings; sumptuously patterned, exotic/Oriental wallcoverings.

 WINDOWS Sumptuous/themed: generously draped, period/exotic curtain styles; swags and tails; grand tiebacks; heraldic-style, metal curtain poles; shaped cornices, valances; starkly modern, minimalist fabric panels.
Blinds: contemporary slatted styles; voluminous festoon styles in romantic sheers.

 FABRICS Exotic/metallics: richly colored silks, satins, brocades, velvets and devoré velvets; gold/metallic-accent prints; shimmery sheers; saris; fur fabric, animal prints; black-and-white graphic prints; PVC, leather.

 FLOORING Luxurious/graphic: solid plush pile carpet; animal print/theme pattern carpet; customized linoleum/woodblock designs; marble effects; faux effect painted floor.

 FURNITURE Theatrical flourish: glass, metal, polished wood for grand, period-style, or ultra-modern/designer pieces; unusual/eclectic materials for focal point armoire, bookcase, dresser; flamboyant, oversized sofa, character chairs with luxurious upholstery; focal point coffee table/chests of drawers.

 LIGHTING Impressive/atmospheric: Venetian glass/crystal-drop chandelier; elaborate, wrought-iron/gilt/glass, period-style central fixtures, lamps/sconces; minimalist contemporary designs; dimmer switches; large pillar candles.

ACCESSORIES Eclectic/ornate: colorful, luxury fabric pillows; animal print, hand-painted/handmade designer lamp shades; candelabra; oversized candles; large glass/pottery vases; gilt/character frame mirror; fringe trims and tassels; art prints; flamboyant plant/flower displays.

▼ *Supremely controlled, the drama of this scheme lies in the subtle influence of Art Deco and serene Oriental style. The perfect balance of black and white and the splendidly theatrical flourish of the window treatment complete the Dramatic effect.*

▲ **A vibrant color scheme** celebrates a Dramatic blend of the rich and exotic, reflecting the diversity of modern style influences.

Sumptuous, jewel-bright fabrics for upholstery and pillows look rich and luxurious.

Decorative MDF (medium-density fiberboard) trims give a striking new edge to cornices and decorative moldings.

Innovative occasional furniture makes a bold Dramatic style statement.

A focal-point rug links the various color elements in the room.

Color-splash flowers complement the bright and bold Dramatic decorative theme.

DRAMATIC FURNISHINGS

If you have more dash than cash – or if you simply like the effect – you can capitalize on the dramatic impact of a stripped or vibrantly painted floor as an alternative to carpet. A formal checkered pattern or faux stone effect will immediately help to define a style or suggest a period look. Consider a marble effect, or a trompe l'oeil border for a less than gracious fireplace, and the possibility of adding a mural or trompe l'oeil detail somewhere to disguise inappropriate features.

You can use special preshaped MDF trims to create exotic cornices and to embellish shelves, baseboards and door surrounds. Use inexpensive muslin or painted calico to line walls or tent a ceiling. Alternatively, rely on a single piece of furniture or a carefully arranged group, together with imaginative soft furnishings, such as a fabulous fabric for upholstery or pillows, to provide the main focus of attention.

Regard flowers and plants as pieces of furniture too – a large specimen plant has the grace and movement of a piece of sculpture, and a diva-sized bouquet of flowers in a generously proportioned vase can take up as much space as an average armchair.

Rich reds, exotically figured patterns and glinting gold detailing add up to a sumptuous scheme. The casually knotted curtain is an inspired flourish – as expected in a Dramatic style living room.

Striking color contrasts and bold stripes transform a pleasant and conventional period sitting room into an individualist's comfortable retreat.

Dramatic fabrics

Dress up windows with romantic or exotic drapes – you can drape a length of a feature fabric over a less expensive fabric, or use it for borders. Pay attention to poles and fittings, and choose them appropriately, as these are an important finishing touch. Enlarge the appearance of a window by extending the curtains on each side of the window frame, and site the hardware as high as possible to allow for a grand sweep to the floor, where the fabric can puddle extravagantly. Formal or informal swags and tails will also make the most of an unremarkable window shape.

Reserve your most sumptuous fabrics for a starring role center stage – a fabulous velvet, brocade or animal print for a sofa, chair seat or pillows. Try mirroring pieces by placing two identically upholstered chairs opposite each other, or try the same trick with pillows or a pair of distinctive table lamp shades, to create a sense of balance and color flow.

Exotic adventures and travelers' tales from another era come to mind in this lovingly created sitting room which, with a stretch of the imagination, could be in the foothills of a distant land.

A controlled explosion of jewel-bright colors and richly textured fabrics has a dramatic impact on the calculatedly calm and spacious neutral tones of the sofa and flooring.

59

STYLE DETAILS

In a Dramatic setting, prudent accessorizing is often required, as a spare look can have the most striking impact, especially with bold, classically inspired schemes or with a strong color or contemporary design theme. However, for an eclectic look, or for many exotic schemes, a myriad of little details can positively enhance the dramatic potential. Each Dramatic style influence and theme will suggest its own finishing touches. Whatever the main influence, the secret of success is to group key pieces – pictures, *objets*, plants and flowers – together, or in such a way that they form a good balance with one another and other elements. Every addition should earn its place in the scheme in some way.

▶ *A curtain treatment based on a heraldic theme has all the hallmarks of Dramatic style. All the detailing – the elaborate pole, gold cord and fringing, and the intricate holdbacks show a real commitment to theatrical effect.*

◀ *Borrowing from the simplicity and discipline of Oriental style, black-and-white accessories make a significant style gesture in this boldly conceived Dramatic room scheme.*

▶ *The clearly defined lines of the Gothic style chair are perfectly complemented by the sinuous curves of the candleholder and classical stone pieces. The contrast between these elements is typical of sensual Dramatic style.*

Create a bedroom that you will enjoy by selecting a style that is an honest reflection of you. Discover the serenity of traditional classic, the comfort of the cottage or the calm of the waterfront. Or show off your romantic flair or your memories of exotic far-off countries. Consider the needs and interests of children as you decorate the bedrooms in which they will play and grow.

Just as in the first section, a summary of each style's important characteristics is found under the headline Style Pointers. Examine the photographs to discover fresh ideas for bedroom furnishings and styling details. Select a familiar style already used in the living areas, or explore the possibilities of a few new styles that work especially well in the bedroom. Change at least one decorating aspect – style, color or pattern – to provide decorating interest in your home, but repeat some elements to maintain a pleasing visual flow.

CLASSIC BEDROOM

Choose a Classic-style bedroom and surround yourself with the serenity of earlier times as you sleep. The glow of polished wood, fine fabrics and gentle lighting create a sense of luxurious comfort.

A restful bedroom where you can relax and let cares slip away is important for everyone, and for many people the look of times gone by epitomizes an atmosphere of quiet calm and peace. With its graceful traditional furniture, rich attention to detail and pretty period accessories, Classic style evokes a less hurried age, and offers a chance to pamper yourself or your guests with a sense of elegant living.

Don't worry if your home has no period details – it's easy to add architectural moldings such as cornicing, or even hang wallpaper trompe l'oeil borders. In a bedroom, large items of furniture – particularly the bed – take precedence: you can dress up the simplest divan with pretty fabrics, and choose reproduction or second-hand wardrobes and chests to continue the period look. Search the family attic and scour antique stores for pretty crystal perfume jars and dainty bedside lamps to complete the Classic ambience.

▲ *A wall covered in a cool gray-blue toile de Jouy makes an elegant and luxurious setting for a Classic bedroom – the fabric is used again for a toning bedcover. A delicately detailed built-in cupboard makes room for an imposing brass bedstead, and a sweep of cream voile dresses up a practical roller blind. Crystal, silver and flowers reflected in a three-sided mirror (inset) create a light, refined look.*

CREATING THE STYLE

Aim for a well-cared-for, elegantly comfortable look, with glossily polished furniture and carefully detailed soft furnishings. Add a delicate cornice, simple coving or a picture rail if your ceiling is high enough. Try to make the room look as big as possible, so plan the decoration in line with its proportions. A pale-colored ceiling maximizes height in any room; as a background in a smaller room, paint walls in soft, receding shades – dusty pinks and beiges, delicate buttermilk or magnolia – and keep woodwork white or pale gloss. Special effects such as lining or marbling are appropriate, but keep them subtle; built-in wardrobes look smaller with door panels or moldings picked out in toning colors. Wallpaper or stencil borders depicting period moldings or pretty floral garlands, at ceiling line or dado height, add period detail to plain walls.

In a more spacious room, wallpapers enhance the look – finely drawn floral or leaf patterns with delicate coloring, toile de Jouy prints or subtle satiny stripes are ideal. To give a really luxurious look, opt for traditional fabric-covered walls, with fabric stapled to battens over thick interlining, and edged with braid.

STYLE POINTERS

 WALLS Pale/soft: soft, unobtrusive matte paints or glazes; refined paint effects such as marbling, stenciling or lining; white or pale gloss woodwork.
Wallpapers: delicate, medium-scale florals; textural damask designs; toile de Jouy-style pictorial prints; elaborate or simple stripes; borders.

 WINDOWS Curtains: prettily swagged or valanced, with finishing details such as rosettes, tassels and trims, and matching bed drapes.
Blinds: Austrian or pleated blinds; roller blinds with braid-trimmed, shaped hems.

 FLOORING Traditional: pale or subtly colored wall-to-wall carpet, plain, self-patterned or textured borders; polished wood.
Rugs: cut Chinese style in soft pastels; tapestries; floral cross-stitch.

 FABRICS Fine: silks, damask, toile de Jouy; 'archive' floral chintzes and linens.

 FURNITURE Period: polished hardwood freestanding pieces; built-in wardrobes with pretty paint finishes or hardwood veneers.
Bed: impressive period styles – four-posters or half testers; carved head and footboards; brass or wrought-iron bedsteads.

 LIGHTING Gentle: brass wall sconces shaded with tiny candle shades; softly lit crystal central chandelier; traditional-style bedside table lamps with pleated silk shades.

 ACCESSORIES Period/elegant: botanical prints; gilt-framed mirrors; silver-backed brushes; crystal perfume bottles; monogrammed or discreetly embroidered bed linen.

With a cool, airy color scheme, this bedroom strikes a different but unmistakably Classic note. A filigree wrought-iron bedstead is an important feature, and elegant glazed built-in cupboards have a detailed paint finish. A tapestry carpet glows softly against the polished wood floor.

Subtly patterned wallpaper and floral print curtains create a warm but elegant background. Highly polished hardwood furniture, with delicate brass handles, provides ample hanging and drawer space. Ornately framed pictures give Classic character to the room. Pretty candlesticks and flowers, together with lace-trimmed bed linen, give the room a lively, period feel.

CLASSIC FURNISHINGS

Focus the room round the bed, which, if possible, should be period style – a bedstead in brass, wrought iron or polished wood. However, there are plenty of ways to customize a plain divan. Fix shoulder-height, reeded or cord-wrapped chunky poles with impressive finials to each corner, and swirl them with fabric; fix a square of molding to the ceiling and hang curtains at each corner for a mock four-poster; or dress a half-corona kit with curtains looped back with rosettes, and a pretty valance.

A matching quilted or fitted bedcover, finished with a bolster or a pile of pillows, gives the bed a thoroughly well-dressed look. At the window, a formal arrangement with a cornice or drapery coordinating with the bed treatment adds a grand touch; if you prefer a pole, choose a traditional polished wood or brass style. Rich trimmings such as fringing and tassels are more suitable than frills.

Freestanding furniture in traditional Georgian or Victorian style can be picked up at auctions or second-hand shops – look for pieces with a fine, rather light style with beading and dainty brass handles, rather than solid, heavy-looking chests and wardrobes.

▼ *The height of Classic elegance, a four-poster creates a dramatic focal point, formally dressed with a swagged valance, curtains and quilted bedspread in cool greens and pink.*

Softly feminine, a dressing table with an oval mirror is silhouetted against the window. A ruffled skirt and frilled top can easily be added to a plain table; protect the top with tempered glass, to reflect pretty matching lamps and silver accessories.

With its beautifully detailed padded headboard, quilted bedcover and gathered canopy, this bed is definitely dressed to impress. A small round bedside table draped with a floor-length cloth holds a porcelain lamp with pleated shade, and fresh and dried flowers.

The brass ring handles and gracefully curving base on this chest of drawers give it a light, pretty look. Many reproduction collections have designs that suit the Classic style.

THE CADOGAN ESTATE   Robert Pearman

Many companies offer collections of reproduction furniture to suit the Classic style, veneered in rosewood, mahogany or cherry. If you prefer built-in furniture, choose a similar veneered finish, or for a lighter look in a small room, a gloss paint finish. Paint details or panels with a subtle contrast to break up a large expanse of cupboards.

A dressing table makes a pretty feature, set with a wood or gilt-framed mirror. Bedside tables can be period style, or dress small round chipboard ones in long cloths. If you have room, a tiny couch, ottoman or upholstered blanket box at the end of the bed is useful; an occasional chair or small tub chair is a smaller alternative.

Lighting is in period style and creates pools of soft light round the room; a crystal chandelier strikes the right note, but keep the wattage low. Wall sconces in brass with little shades provide discreet illumination; porcelain or brass-based lamps with parchment or pleated silk shades are ideal beside the bed.

67

STYLE DETAILS

Gilt-framed watercolors, botanical prints, silhouette portraits and mirrors decorate the walls of a Classic bedroom; picture bows make a nice addition. Make a collection of old silver-backed brushes and dainty perfume sprays to adorn a dressing table or chest top. Bed linen can be decorative but not too frilly – plain white or cream cotton with satin-stitched monograms or subtle ribbon lace is in keeping with the style. Scent the air with bowls of fresh flowers and potpourri in silver dishes.

▲ *Silver-backed brushes and pretty bottles catch the light on the highly polished surface of a period-style dressing table.*

▲ *For a Classic finishing touch, hang pictures from large butterfly bows, balanced with dainty china plates; a finely pleated paper shade picks up the blue of the padded headboard.*

▲ *Discreetly embellished bed linen in white, ivory and beige is a hallmark of the Classic bedroom. Subtle satin stitching, fine piping or fagoting should be self-colored or at least neutral for a simple but elegant effect.*

▶ *Silver-plated candlesticks in a classically restrained design are topped with plain and simple parchment shades.*

COUNTRY COTTAGE BEDROOM

*The fresh simplicity of Country Cottage style strikes the right
note for a calm and restful bedroom scheme, and works as well
in a modern town house as in a rural setting.*

A buttercup yellow color scheme, simple wooden furniture and white lacy bed linen give this cottage bedroom a cheerful, sunny air. The imposing brass bed, backed by its padded floral panel, and a pile of striking hatboxes, add character and detail.

A small bedroom chair with billowing roses and a flowing floor-length skirt makes ideal occasional seating in any cottage bedroom.

The essence of cottage style is a sense of peace – set apart from the noise and sophistication of modern city life. It's the perfect style for a bedroom, helping you to relax and unwind for the night. Colors are soft and light with plenty of florals, evoking flower-filled meadows and cottage gardens.

Unpretentious and rustic, the Country Cottage look can be an economical option – furniture is an easy mix of secondhand pieces, such as old chests of drawers and brass bedsteads, or chunky pine – readily available and well priced. The style suits even tiny rooms, creating a cozy and comfortable haven with simple furniture and dainty accessories.

69

CREATING THE STYLE

The charm of a Country Cottage-style bedroom is in its simple, old-fashioned look. Pretty colors and delicate patterns are mixed with well-worn basic furniture and traditional touches such as dried flowers and old china.

Walls are pale – choose plain flat paints in white, cream or pastels, perhaps with a decorative border or stenciled motif; or pick a flower-scattered paper as a basis for the scheme. Keep paintwork white or choose a soft tone from the wallpaper – pinks, blue-gray or pale olive. Flooring should not be too luxurious – stick to pale, neutral shades.

Restrict the furniture to the basics – the bed should take center stage, dressed to invite with lacy bed linen or perhaps a patchwork quilt. Details are ideally homemade, so needn't be expensive – embroidered pillows, dried flowers and pictures all add the essential touches.

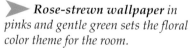 *Fresh spring green and white contrast with the splendor of this dramatic bed frame. Touches of lace, dainty stenciled motifs and a flowery quilted bedspread create an airy, welcoming room.*

STYLE POINTERS

 WALLS Pale/pastels: plain, or use paint effects such as sponging or colorwashing for the illusion of rough plaster; delicate touches of stenciling can add detail.
Wallpapers: pale, narrow stripes or small motifs; florals or leafy patterns, trellis designs.

 WINDOWS Curtains: simple on a wood or metal pole; frilled valances; single swag and tail drapes; lace panels or voile curtains, plain or flower-sprigged; traditional fabric or cord tiebacks.
Blinds: Austrian blinds; roller blinds with a shaped hem.

 FLOORING Natural/pale: bare wood floorboards, stained or painted white; natural fiber matting; carpet in neutral or soft colors; dainty-patterned carpet.
Rugs: homemade tufted or cross-stitch rugs in toning colors, rag rugs, pale dhurries.

 FABRICS Pretty: cotton or linen florals, country motifs; simple checks and stripes; calico, muslin, lace.

 FURNITURE Simple: wicker or cane, mahogany, oak or country pine; painted or limed wood.
Bed: brass, iron or chunky wood; four-posters.

 LIGHTING Cozy: period glass tulip shades or small brass chandeliers; wall candle-style sconces; table lamps, oil lamps and candles.

 ACCESSORIES Pretty/period: floral china washbowls and pitchers; embroidered cushions and pillows; colored glass; candlesticks; dried flower arrangements; watercolors or flower prints in wood frames.

Rose-strewn wallpaper in pinks and gentle green sets the floral color theme for the room.
A simple window treatment of plain white valanced curtains, with a fine edging of soft brown, keeps the room light and bright, allowing other stronger elements to take center stage.
White painted floorboards are an economical treatment in a room that gets light use. A blue-gray rug adds comfort and color contrast.
Floral fabric on the headboard, pillows and ottoman echoes the rose theme, creating softness and a feeling of comfort.
Dark wood in the chest of drawers and bedside table provides a rich contrast to the pale tones and pretty colors of the walls and fabrics.

COUNTRY COTTAGE FURNISHINGS

The bed takes center stage in a Country Cottage-style bedroom. Traditional designs in brass or wrought iron give the room individuality, but you can customize a simple divan by adding a prettily upholstered headboard and a lace-edged valance. Lacy or embroidered bed linen has the right period look, but a floral cotton duvet set is a good modern equivalent. Pretty embroidered pillows or a bolster add a welcoming softness.

A cane chair with a cushion is a useful addition, as is an upholstered chair, if you have space. Freestanding furniture is more in keeping than built-in wardrobes, but if you already have built-in units you could soften the stark look of melamine doors, for example, by adding moldings and panels of wallpaper. Ideally, a chest of drawers and wardrobe in polished wood are all you need; for added storage, place a wooden or old tin chest, or fabric-covered blanket box,

at the end of the bed or under the window. Beside the bed, a small wooden table can be left bare or draped with a toning cloth or piece of old lace to hold a simple pottery or brass lamp with a pretty shade.

At the window, there are plenty of options. Choose flower-patterned curtains trimmed with frills and topped with a ruffled valance for a traditional Country look. For a fresh, light look, opt for a roller blind for privacy, then add billowing voile curtains, in sherbet shades or scattered with wild flowers. You may choose to play the window down with simple calico or striped ticking curtains on a pole.

Choose lighting that is either unobtrusive or a period feature. Simple plaster sconces, painted to match the wall, can suit the newer Country style; pretty brass wall lamps with tiny candle shades, or a period-style central fixture, give a more traditional air.

◀ *A textured paper for the dado painted in rose pink echoes the blooming cabbage rose and ribbon paper above. Make dainty little drawstring bags in pretty prints or lace for potpourri or jewelry, and hang a dried rose pomander for fragrance.*

▶ *Lovingly covered in rose-printed paper, these boxes with their smart gilt corners, ribbon and tassel trims are ideal accessories to add detail and interest to a cottage bedroom. Fresh roses complete the theme and scent the air.*

▲ Pile on the
flowers by
covering pillows
in a medley of
floral fabrics, all
exquisitely piped
and frilled.

▼ Crisp red and white puts a fresh
slant on Country style. A filigree
trellis wallpaper makes a neat
background for a crisp floral print in red
and green on white, used on tiny frilled
curtains, an elaborate headboard and
quilted bedspread. Hinged rods swing
away from the window in daytime to
show off a pretty window profile in the
dormer recess – a typical cottage feature.

▲ This unashamedly feminine
room focuses attention on the
window, lavishing it with frilled
curtains and valance, and matching
tiebacks. The sky blue delphinium-
print fabric conjures up summer
afternoons in the cottage garden.

STYLE DETAILS

Create an atmosphere of old-world charm in a Country Cottage bedroom with ingeniously placed details. Fragile antique textiles can be displayed as table covers or draped at the window; mount a dramatic dried flower arrangement to decorate a wall. Use drifts of decoupage or stenciled flowers to highlight features of the room. A small vase of fresh flowers is always perfectly in keeping, or scent the room with aromatic candles in china or brass candlesticks.

▶ *Show off a pretty antique shawl or embroidered cloth to full effect by using it to dress up a window. This artless arrangement is threaded through two curtain pole rings hung above the window, and is set off perfectly by the lace panel and blue sponged wall.*

▼ *Decoupage roses and ribbons cleverly suggest a headboard on the wall above a bed, making a frame for peach and dainty white lace pillows – tiny touches that are vital elements of a Country bedroom.*

▶ *Sweetly reminiscent of an age of true romance, this wistfully romantic heart with its lavender, berries and rosebuds makes the perfect wall decoration for a Country bedroom.*

A ROMANTIC BEDROOM

Set the scene for romance with a pale swirl of voile,
whimsical gilded cherubs, garlands of ivy and orange
blossom – a bedroom where Romeo meets Juliet.

Indulge your flights of fancy and create a haven of romance in your bedroom – a place to lose yourself in your dreams, with the harsh realities of life shut firmly out. The look is light and fanciful, with dramatic devices borrowed straight from the stage – drapery or architectural details painted on the wall, a ceiling gleaming with stenciled stars or paper cutout doves. It's also essentially simple; avoid heavy florals and intricate frills, and keep the backdrop pale and fairly plain, with lots of pure white, or misty grays and creams. The bed has the star role – look for something a little bit special, perhaps with a carved mahogany headboard or swirly wrought iron, or else add a simple airy drape from a gilded or leafy coronet.

▲ *In a romantic bedroom, a feature such as a trailing ivy coronet set against a sweeping bed drape and lacy pillows can be a starting point for further imaginative touches. Complement a scene such as this by choosing details carefully – the framed picture with its ribbon lacing and twisted wire hearts (inset) adds texture without intrusive color.*

CREATING THE STYLE

The dramatically romantic bedroom has a pure, almost virginal look to it – a clean, Classic style against which feminine lace and flowers have a sweet, vulnerable poignancy.

Aim for an airy, spacious look, with not too many patterns. Walls can be painted in white, cream or dove gray, or you could pick a delicate cloudy pastel such as palest mauve or blue. Soft paint effects, such as colorwashing and sponging in watery cool colors, can give the effect of the sky at dusk or dawn. Trompe l'oeil effects such as classical columns and paneling, or mock stone work, build on the theatrical effect.

Wallpaper should be similarly pale, featuring small classical motifs – laurel wreaths or gracefully scrolling patterns. Look for borders featuring dancing cherubs, hearts and flowers or mock plaster molding, to add a touch of detail to plain walls. Stick to pale colors in gloss or eggshell for woodwork, or strip it down and wax for an antique look.

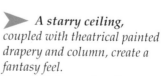 More traditional but just as inviting, a dark wood four-poster hung with ethereal white voile curtains dominates the room. Dainty accessories – framed miniatures, frilled lace pillows, a tiny heart pillow and a huge bowl of roses hint at romance.

STYLE POINTERS

 WALLS Pale/soft: light, airy tones in flat or eggshell; paint effects – trompe l'oeil, colorwash, dragging, sponging, stenciled motifs with touches of gilt.
Wallpapers: small dainty sprigs or classical motifs on a light background; self patterns; toile de Jouy designs; whimsical or classical borders.

 WINDOWS Curtains: loose folds of voile or muslin draped over a pole, or simple curtains on a pole.
Blinds: functional roller blind to block light and provide privacy, with prettily shaped hem.

 FLOORING Unobtrusive: stripped boards, limed or stained; natural floorcoverings; plain or textured wall-to-wall carpet in neutral colors.
Rugs: flat-weave rugs in pale colors, sheepskin, Swedish-style cross-stitch rugs in restrained colors.

 FURNITURE Period style: antique, neo-classical, modern Gothic or Swedish style in polished woods or distressed paint effects, metals, stone.
Grand bed: period bed frames or four-posters in brass, iron or wood; half tester or coronet.

 LIGHTING Atmospheric: candelabra in crystal or wrought iron; shaded wall lamps; dainty gilt or brass candle sconces.

ACCESSORIES Whimsical: gilt-framed mirrors, gilded cherubs, dainty silhouettes; white porcelain, fluted glass; white flowers, trailing greenery.

A starry ceiling, coupled with theatrical painted drapery and column, create a fantasy feel.
A graceful weeping fig placed close to the bed suggests a romantic fairy glade.
An imposing bed frame in brass and white enamel looks inviting against its imaginative backdrop.
Softly draped white voile gently filters the light through the window.
A snowy lace bedspread and matching tablecloth add to the romantic bedroom atmosphere.

76

ROMANTIC STYLE FURNISHINGS

The bed is the starting point in almost any bedroom, but needs special emphasis for this dramatically romantic style. An imposing four-poster in wood or metal makes a real impact, but you can dress up a simple bed with an ornate headboard, a coronet, or even just a length of muslin looped across the wall. Add a twist of ivy or loose branches of mock orange blossom, but keep it casual rather than tightly contrived.

Bed linen should be white or cream, with intricate detailing such as lace, drawn threadwork and ribbons. Touches of blue on white have a fresh, classic feel and make a good contrast to dark woods. Pile up sleeping and dainty pillows for an inviting look.

Keep other furniture to a minimum so as not to draw attention away from the bed. Period-style chests and wardrobes in dark polished wood, or in the pale faded paint typical of Swedish furniture, are ideal. As an individual touch, a stone urn topped with a circle of glass makes a Dramatic bedside table. A wrought-iron chair has a similarly austere look; if you have

room, add an iron side table topped with glass as a dressing table. For a softer look, you could dress a round chipboard table in a long, white damask or lace-trimmed cloth.

Filmy voile and muslin are almost fundamental to the Dramatic look, and come in lovely classical prints or scattered with stars and fleurs-de-lis. But there are also plenty of heavier fabrics that would continue the theme if you want more substantial curtains or a matching bedspread. Look for cotton prints in pale green, primrose

▶ Gilded cupids and gold cord supporting a drift of voile frame the head of the bed, and set the theme of fairytale romance.

◀ Black provides a strong contrast to pale buttery yellow and white, and strikes a note of sophisticated formality in this pretty scheme. Classical cherubs cavort across the headboard, bedcover and small pillows, with unusual black-and-white spotted pillows. The black iron lamps with flying ribbons are bold but pretty, standing out in silhouette against the pale background colors.

◄ *'Something borrowed, something blue' – the classic blue-and-white scheme has hints of romance, teamed with fresh flowers and pure white linen. On the wall, a blue-and-white floral scrolled fabric edged with braid adds a sense of luxury and comfort.*

▲ *In a strikingly modern interpretation of an ancient theme, a contemporary iron four-poster is set against a classic toile de Jouy design in smoky lilac and dressed in tumbling swathes of mauve silk and creamy crinkle cotton. The window has a similarly casual treatment.*

or powder blue, featuring formal swags of fruit and flowers, swirling acanthus leaves and capering cupids; simple checks or stripes in white and cool blues or lilac, crunchy natural cottons or fine flowing silks – always in pale watery tones – would work well too. Upholster a small armchair in an intricate, pretty brocade or smooth, pale velvet.

Plan lighting for dramatic effect. A crystal chandelier or iron candelabra looks effective, but two decorative wall lights flanking the bed will give a soft glow; a tall, ornate Gothic candlestick in a corner adds drama.

Set a large mirror in an ornate gilt frame on the wall, or make your own by twisting a plain frame with ivy and spraying it with gold paint. Plaster wall plaques of amorous gods and goddesses would suit the theme; gilt cherubs are easy to find in gift shops. Frame pictures in antique gilt or simple black – look for Marie Antoinette-style engravings, dainty silhouettes or Pre-Raphaelite maidens in flowing robes. Arrange crystal bottles and silver-backed brushes on a dressing table, together with a vase of flowers and ferns.

◄ *In this Dramatic scheme, the cool colors of stone and marble, and the classical drapery at the window and over the bed, call to mind the ancient Greeks and Romans, with their fables of amorous deities.*

STYLE DETAILS

Evoke the stuff of dreams with details that hint at the romance of fables and fairies. Keep them light, airy and whimsical – candleholders for a 'Faerie Queene', pale spindly chairs, a tub of feathery greens and white baby's breath, and swaths of filmy fabric. Scented candles in dainty holders complete the picture.

Create this bridal garland of blossoms and greenery, to entwine a bed frame or swag a table.

Cherubs find their way onto a huge variety of accessories – the flickering light of a candle will show up the chubby curves of this miniature cupid.

Pretty gilt candleholders fit for a royal boudoir will add a twinkling gleam to your bedside.

In this charming bedroom, a romantically draped window is complemented by a pretty display of gilt-edged porcelain and clouds of baby's breath.

WATERFRONT BEDROOM

*Fresh as a sea breeze, the waterfront bedroom is at one
with its surroundings. Its color schemes celebrate the subtle tones of
the sea and sky, and nautical themes inspire its styling details.*

A feeling of light – that special light, with an elusive quality found only by the sea – plays an important role in the waterfront bedroom, where it bathes every surface with its subtle tones. This influence is reflected in the choice of color schemes and furnishings and in the simple style of the furnishings – in keeping with the unassuming character of a seaside cottage.

You can capture the essential freshness and understated look of a real waterfront bedroom wherever you live, and compensate for the lack of an authentic location with clever

▲ *The sound of the surf and the calling of gulls is an evocative image, one that this bedroom scheme would conjure up, even without seeing the view from the window. Gentle shades of marine blue and white, simple furniture and charming nautical details epitomize the charming waterfront bedroom.*

lighting and colors that draw on the subtle hues of the coastline and seashore. Choose from the soft and muted blues and grayed greens, sandy yellows and stone shades that capture the subtleties of the northern seashores, or go for the sharper and more robust colors of warmer, southern climes.

CREATING THE LOOK

A practical, uncluttered approach with simple painted walls, weathered wood and essential furniture and furnishings in natural materials, head the list of basic requirements for the waterfront bedroom. The look is spare – even minimal – but the atmosphere is reassuringly cozy and comfortable; a haven complemented by charmingly simple accessories, all chosen to enhance the waterfront theme.

A soft shade of blue or aqua, applied to walls as a colorwash or paint effect wallcovering, helps to establish the theme. Alternatively, start with walls in a natural white, to simulate rustic whitewash. Collect coastal theme pictures from magazines and brochures to help you decide whether you

want to create a gentle, almost Scandinavian look, capture the ambience of a traditional, sunny seaside resort, or go for the deeper colors of a more distant coastal location. Then you can temper the quality of the colors accordingly.

Strip and seal floorboards, or paint them a flat-finish color and add rush mats or soft cotton rugs. Woodwork and furniture is simple Country style, with a limed or distressed finish, or simple, mellow pine.

Nautical-style lighting is functional and attractive, and underlines the waterfront theme. Look for designs based on traditional oil lamps and bulkhead wall fixtures in chrome, brass or white, and simple candle wall sconces.

STYLE POINTERS

 WALLS Soft color/plain: colorwashed effects; distressed, natural/painted or limed wood tongue-and-groove paneling and woodwork; marine stencil/painted motifs.

 WINDOWS Uncluttered: simple curtain styles such as flowing voile or muslin panels; windowsill or long length on rods or wood/metal poles.
Blinds: slatted wood styles; plain roller blinds; traditional wooden shutters.

 FABRICS Cottons/linens/woolens: plain white; soft, woven stripes or checks, particularly in shades of blue and white; deck-chair stripes; calico; waffle cotton; marine motif prints; woolen blankets and throws; patchwork quilts in muted colors

 FLOORING Stripped boards/rugs: mellow, natural wood; area rugs in sisal, coconut matting, woven cotton; rag rugs.

 FURNITURE Rustic/simple: country-style pine or plain, period-style iron bed frame; traditional painted or distressed finish wooden chests of drawers, country-style upright wooden chairs, bedside tables, wooden bench; matching wardrobe or fitted alcove cupboards with paneled doors and iron latchhook; cane/willow armchair or slipcovered style.

 LIGHTING Nautical influence/lanterns: hanging storm lantern, bulkhead fixtures, candle sconces.

 ACCESSORIES Seashore/rustic: driftwood/seashell pictures or mirror frames, carved wooden sea birds, model ships and boats, lighthouse, fishing paraphernalia.

Brilliant tropical sky and deep sea blue is a dazzling combination with clear, bright white. A porthole-shaped mirror and decorative globe give clues that warm coastal waters were the starting point for this simple but powerful color scheme.

The atmospheric color scheme seems to be filled with hazy light and captures the peace and solitude of a misty coastal scene.

Soft blue details *evoke the cool blue-grays so typical of northern seascapes.*

White painted floorboards *are a plain and simple waterfront feature.*

A simple white cotton bedspread *balances beautifully with white painted wood.*

Ornaments with a nautical theme *acknowledge the source of inspiration for the scheme, and provide a subtle finishing touch.*

WATERFRONT FURNISHINGS

Waterfront furnishings are charming, pretty, practical – and pared down – fussiness is inappropriate; the only extras are key accessories to complement the theme.

The bed itself beckons as a blissful haven. In hot weather a pure white cotton coverlet looks cool and inviting, but as the air grows chilly, cosy layers are essential – and decorative. Here you can develop the waterfront theme with color; piling on blues, grays and greens and soft sand tones as highlights in cotton quilts and simple wool blankets and throws.

Bed linen and pillows may be decorated with seashell stitchery, or with appliqué or printed boats and other maritime motifs. Alternatively, aim for a pristine look with fresh, pure white, aqua, or palest blue cotton. Little splashes of red, golden sand and sunshine yellow appearing in deck-chair stripes, patchwork designs, slipcovers and fabric accessories such as cotton rugs and little drawstring bags, can lift the color and add a cheerful shoreline feel.

Window treatments are low-key and easy on the eye – practical painted wood shutters, flung open invitingly to the breeze, have timeless, romantic appeal. Happily, if your view is not of the tumbling surf and the windswept beach, sheer voiles or muslin drapes are just as evocative. Use these or fine cotton fabrics as billowing full-length curtains, with or without shutters, and over simple slatted blinds.

Utterly simple, the graceful lines of the iron bed complement the crisp white bed linen and casually knotted bed drape. The red stripe throw is an inspired touch; a visual reference to seaside striped taffy, lifebuoy markings and gaily colored deck chairs.

On a seashore theme, sandy yellow and pale blue create an imaginative setting for a fantasy mural in a child's room. Collections of seashells and pebbles and a splendid model lighthouse complement the decorations.

A single wooden sea bird, perched high on a ledge, strikes exactly the right note to complement your waterfront bedroom. Themed accessories – handcrafted with a distressed, rustic finish – are usually inexpensive and have a unique, simple charm.

Beach-combed treasure has endless style potential. Here, where rustic simplicity is the keynote, a seashell frieze becomes a decorative focal point.

Hand-stitched quilts are very welcome in the waterfront bedroom. In shades of blue and gentle misty tones, they complement worn wood and muted colors.

85

WATERFRONT DETAILS

Witty and pretty, waterfront accessories and details really set the scene and, because the style of the bedroom is so simple, they work as high-profile finishing touches.

Seashells, pebbles and fantastic driftwood forms are time-honored beachcombing treasures. As simple arrangements – drifted into a corner of the bedroom or displayed as a collection on a table or shelf, they look subtle, simple and beautiful. You can create seashell borders and patterns on mirror and picture frames, or use them as shelf edge trims. A piece of driftwood can become a sculptural jewelry tree, hung with necklaces and bangles, while seaglass 'pebbles' would look pretty in a glass dish filled with water to show their colors. Place them on a windowsill or dressing table where they can catch the light.

Wooden bird carvings, model boats and lighthouses have a natural charm, as do memorabilia and collectibles such as phials of colored sand, antique seaside mementoes and marine prints.

Bunches of sea lavender and other coastal plants look splendid arranged in simple stone vases or pots, displayed at floor level or on a small table. Mix these traditional details with more modern accessories such as beautiful glass bottles of oils and pretty marine-scented candles.

The outlook is sunny, and possibly Mediterranean. The vibrant, colorwashed walls, starfish mosaic appliqué pillow and vivid flowers celebrate a pleasantly warm waterfront theme.

Models on a nautical theme abound, so searching for accessories to suit a waterfront bedroom can be rewarding, especially when you find a treasure that fits the theme as perfectly as this tinware lighthouse.

White on white – using texture and quiet, neutral tones for interest – suits this theme well. Here, the laced lamp shade brings a ship's sails to mind – a theme echoed by the little model sailing boat.

Distressed wood is almost an essential in the waterfront bedroom. This rustic cupboard is a versatile piece of furniture and, painted white and teamed with blue, is perfect in its setting.

EXOTIC BEDROOM

*Rich, earthy colors and natural textures make an unusual
and satisfying basis for an Exotic bedroom scheme,
with African and Asian influences.*

The look of an Exotic style bedroom can range through a global spectrum of colors, patterns and moods – from the brilliant colors of Indian silks to the subtle textures of African baskets and earth pots; but the general feel is relaxed and casual, with touches of intricate detail and rich color. The wealth of colorful and interesting items from exotic places, which are readily available in department stores and specialty shops, can provide you with the starting point for your Exotic bedroom. You can add to these with souvenirs of locally made handicrafts brought back from holidays abroad.

The influence of design and style from all parts of the world can be seen in the latest trends in homewares and interior design products, so you can easily put together a scheme for an Exotic style bedroom. If you wish, choose a single theme for the room by angling the look toward one part of the world – the African countries, for example, or India; but an eclectic mix of styles can work just as well.

▲ *Bold and beautiful, a simple fabric
bed drape in shades of burnt orange
and fresh spring green make a clear
reference to Exotic design without
fussiness. A wirework lantern, wall
border and wrought-iron chair echo the
tracery in the design. A whimsical
elephant candle sconce (inset) picks up
the color theme again.*

87

CREATING THE STYLE

Aim for a rustic, simple look in general, although rich colors and textures are also part of the look, particularly if you are going for a Middle Eastern or Indian look. For a cool, tropical look, creamy walls and dark-stained woodwork make a good setting. Warm peachy shades, dull ochre or russet red, brushed on in big loose strokes, recalls rough limed plaster, or you could give the room a Caribbean flavor with zingy pastels such as mango orange and pineapple yellow. A hand-painted or stenciled border round doors and windows – simple flowers and leaves, or dots, squiggles and chevrons – adds a tribal feel.

If you prefer wallcoverings, there are plenty of designs to set the scene. Richly colored Eastern designs featuring elephants and bejeweled Maharajahs re-create ancient splendors; or choose a handprint-effect, or swirling floral or paisley designs; for a more primitive look, opt for earthy naturals with loosely geometric or abstract designs. Choose toning colors in a matte finish for paintwork, or strip and stain to a rich wood sheen.

Covering the walls with fabric gives a romantic tented effect: look for lengths of African or Indian printed cotton to drape over curtain poles fixed on the wall above the bed or stapled to wooden battens; mix designs but restrict the color range to keep the effect restful.

Stripped wooden floorboards, stained to a dark mahogany finish or kept cool and pale, are an ideal finish. Alternatively, choose a woven floorcovering of jute, coir or sisal in natural shades or subtle colors; fitted carpet should be discreetly neutral. All these floor treatments make a good background for vibrantly patterned Exotic-style dhurries and rugs.

 Warm but gentle colors in tones of cream, peach, terra-cotta and soft ochre are blended to infuse the room with a soft glow.
The Moorish style patterned bedspread and toning pillows are typical of the Exotic look.
Natural textures, such as the unvarnished wooden bed, with its simple cased curtains, and the woven floorcovering provide the desired casual effect.
Delicate glass and china accessories in the alcove, and the impressive carving of the chair and bedside table add the finishing touches.

STYLE POINTERS

 WALLS Chalky/rough: loosely washed, soft earthy colors in flat paints, with colorful contrasts in matte, painted or stained woodwork; block-printed simple borders.
Wallpapers: rhythmic ethnic designs in vegetable/mineral dyes – naturals, indigo, russet, terra-cotta and ochre; swirling Eastern designs and detailed picture patterns of exotic animals or birds.

 WINDOWS Curtains: simply hung panels of fabric, sometimes contrast-lined, on rustic iron, wood or bamboo poles; filmy natural muslin and voile; loose swaths of sari silk looped over pole; tassels, silk or jute ropes.
Blinds: cane roll-up style; wooden-slatted venetians; pleated, textured paper blinds.

 FLOORING Basic: natural finishes – wood or woven jute and sisal, in neutrals or soft colors; plain wall-to-wall carpet in similar shades.
Rugs: flat woven dhurries, kilims, Persian or Turkish tufted rugs, embroidered felt or Greek goatskin.

 FABRICS Vigorous patterns: batik, ikat weaves; mud-resist patterns; tribal patchwork; simple embroideries and appliqué; filmy voile or muslin; rich sari silks.

 FURNITURE Hand-worked: heavy, dark wood with peasant-style decoration; simple ironwork; rattan and bamboo, softened with cushions.
Bed: simple iron or wood bed frame – slatted pine styles, limed or stained; cane headboards.

LIGHTING Primitive: iron candelabra and sconces; beaten tin lamp bases with simple parchment shades; hanging brass, tin or glass lanterns; decorative iron, wood or stone candlesticks.

 ACCESSORIES Handcrafted: terra-cotta and stone pots; mosaic mirrors, richly decorated appliqué textiles; hand-beaten and forged metal items; natural objects such as pebbles and seed pods.

▲ *Deeper in tone and bolder in style, the look here is distinctly exotic. A rich red wall, decorated with bands of gold, makes a grand backdrop for a precious gold-embroidered hanging. More red and gold fabrics are draped above the headboard to create a glamorous corona, which combines with polished wood and the huge swirls of a paisley duvet to dazzle the eye with opulence.*

Exotic Style Furnishings

If you are buying a new bed, look for a rustic style, one with hand-carved bedposts or a simple iron frame; head and footboards in decorative cane or bamboo also suit the look. A simple pine slatted bed can be dressed up with exotic hangings and textiles to become the focal point of the room. Drape a textured throw over a plain wooden headboard, or make a slipcover for an old headboard in a lively exotic print or even mock leopardskin. Bed linen in easy-care fabrics is available in lots of exciting primitive-style prints; or go for simple white or cream cotton enlivened with appliqué and embroidery. A pile of pillows scattered on the bed provides an opportunity for interesting textiles and rich details such as tassels and trimmings.

Furniture has a chunky, solid look, often with hand-tooled decorative details, but practical bamboo and cane, sometimes stained in rich dark green, russet or blue, is also ideal for smaller items such as bedside tables and occasional chairs.

Stain a plain, modern wardrobe with a dark finish, and add surface detail with brass upholstery nails in simple patterns. A tented fabric wardrobe is another economical alternative, which you can dress up with tassels and richly colored fabrics. Eastern-style chests of drawers, in gleaming dark woods with lots of brass details are available in stores. Or replace the plain handles of an existing chest with fluffy tassels or simple iron handles.

Keep the window treatment simple and effective. Wooden-slatted venetians are ideal for excluding light, and come in a range of stains to match your scheme; add a simple muslin curtain on an iron rod for daytime privacy, or make very simple curtain panels in a big, vibrant

▲ Turn a simple fabric wardrobe into a bedouin tent for a peaceful hideaway. Add rich and cozy hangings inside, dangling tassels and a pile of cushions for an oasis of peace.

▲ Gleaming gold stars on the wall and hand-carved mahogany furniture set off the opulent collection of fabrics used to dress this Exotic style daybed. Damasks, gilded prints and brocades, betasseled and baubled, reflect the light from a brass and glass lantern.

◄ An inscrutable mandarin and a stack of chests with elaborate brass fittings give this room a distinctly Oriental flavor. The look is heightened by the rich red hangings and green walls. A tatami mat and a paper lantern complete the effect.

print, edged with a brilliant cotton fringe or pom-pon braid. Look for fabrics with the soft but rich colors of natural dyes – terra-cotta, indigo, rose madder and olive – in rhythmic, semigeometric repeating patterns, swirling stylized flowers or batik-effect prints. For an exotic Eastern boudoir, make curtains from brilliantly colored sari lengths, and drape another length over the pole so the colors show up against the light.

When choosing lighting, rustic-looking candelabra, pierced metal or simple glass lanterns all have the right Exotic look, and create a soft glow. Bedside lamps can be polished brass or tin with big coolie shades, or simple iron bases with tall, narrow paper shades. Wall sconces in beaten metal or iron shed a pretty, quiet light, and there is a huge variety of suitable candlesticks available in similar materials.

Mirrors framed with mosaic, rough wood or beaten metal are all in perfect style in the Exotic bedroom. Stand a couple of huge terra-cotta pots on top of the wardrobe, and fill a large pot in a corner with hazel twigs or exotic seed heads and grasses.

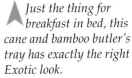 *Just the thing for breakfast in bed, this cane and bamboo butler's tray has exactly the right Exotic look.*

Earth browns and pale creams set an elegant neutral scheme for an Exotic bedroom with a strong Indian theme. A beautiful canework bed forms the centerpiece, complemented by a wooden-slatted venetian blind, a finely carved wood screen and a British Raj style ceiling fan.

STYLE DETAILS

Look for colorful dishes in glazed ceramic or papier mâché to hold jewelry, and beautifully detailed baskets to hold piles of scarves. Drape strings of brightly colored glass beads over a mirror on a chest for an exotic feel. Pretty wind chimes or shell mobiles add a dreamy, romantic sound as they catch the breeze at the window, and perfumed candles or incense evoke the heady atmosphere of the East.

Tiny details that catch the eye are typical of Exotic decoration – gilt and pearl droplets draw attention to the exquisite gold embroidery on this hanging.

Create an arrangement with a satisfying array of different woods for a visual and tactile feast. Here, the rough texture of the plant holder, filled with pale, exotic lilies, contrasts with the lovingly polished bowls and oiled table.

Practical and economical, easy-care polycotton bed linen comes in a dazzling array of vibrant patterns to suit the most global of tastes. For an authentic look, mix different prints together.

Pots like these with their robust and uninhibited designs give life and vitality to any room. Group them on top of a wardrobe or chest, or set them in a corner on polished floorboards or woven jute flooring.

SOFT CONTEMPORARY NURSERY

Light and bright with fresh colors and pretty pattern details, the soft contemporary nursery combines practical features with imaginative touches, to make it a comforting place for little ones.

The Soft Contemporary nursery is an easygoing room, where a feeling for uncluttered space is enhanced by a simple, bright color scheme, practical storage ideas and a relaxed approach to styling. It is a style that does not rely too heavily on coordinates or a particular theme for effect, but more on a flexible mix of colors, fabrics and furniture. The result is a comfortable, welcoming scheme that can be easily adapted or added to as your baby grows.

Since the look is basically low-key, furniture and furnishings can be a charming mix of modern and traditional styles. The trick is to balance different elements through color and pattern; a prettily draped antique cradle or crib will look perfectly at ease with practical, modern storage units if you balance its impact, perhaps with an equally pretty window dressing and accessories.

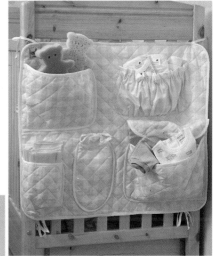

◄ *The look is pretty without being over-sweet, and the teddy bear theme is understated – all hallmarks of the Soft Contemporary nursery. Practical features include the comfortable nursing chair and attractive storage ideas. Hanging pocket panels (inset) are a must in most nurseries; they suit most schemes when made of gingham.*

CREATING THE STYLE

Busy patterns and bold color combinations are out of style in the Soft Contemporary nursery, but there are always pattern details and colorful diversions to interest a young baby.

As with any nursery, practicalities and safety are paramount. Choose flooring that is warm to touch and nonslip – best for crawling toddlers and infant play – in natural wood effects, or vinyl tiles with nonslip rugs, or choose soft wall-to-wall fitted carpet. Keep hot radiator surfaces out of reach behind a radiator cover; you can paint it to match the scheme, and it provides a useful shelf space.

Storage solutions are flexible. Built-in or freestanding painted or pale wood cupboards suit the style, as do securely fixed open shelves with pretty fretwork or fabric edge trims. You can hide potential clutter on shelves behind a curtain or pretty roll-up blind, stacked in wicker baskets or simple plastic containers.

Paint walls in soft solid colors to create a spacious look, or team plains with a dado or border in a low-key nursery design. Dividing the walls in this way helps focus on the lower level, at childs' eye height. The wall treatment should be sufficiently simple to allow for details and accessories – pictures, a frieze, wall pockets or a shelf feature – to be added at a later stage without overcrowding the effect. Stripes or checks are also useful additions to the scheme, since they can help to balance or coordinate the look.

STYLE POINTERS

 WALLS Light/soft pattern: pastel tints and mid-strength solids; soft paint effects; wallpapers with coordinated borders and dados; wood paneling; discreet use of nursery motifs, murals, stenciled motifs.

 WINDOWS Simple/pretty: fabric blinds; matching/coordinating curtains; informal curtain heading styles; painted wood curtain pole; shaped cornices; novelty tiebacks.

 FABRICS Unfussy/nursery motifs: washable cotton-mix checks, stripes and solids; motif prints for curtains, bed linen and accessories.

 FLOORING Practical/comfortable: easy-to-clean wall-to-wall carpet; pale polished wood or simulated wood; cork/vinyl tiles; nonslip rugs/cotton throws.

 FURNITURE Informal/versatile: simple, natural or painted wood crib; light wood finish or painted built-in or freestanding cupboard/hanging storage; chest of drawers/changing pad surface; decorative/practical shelves; wood or wicker toy/storage chest; comfortable low-seated nursing chair; child's table and chair; radiator cover.

 LIGHTING Soft/diffused: hanging pendant lights; sconces; dimmer switches.

 ACCESSORIES Practical/pretty: in fabrics to coordinate/color match scheme; wall pockets; tidy bags; crib set; chair slipcover; quilt/throw; novelty pillows; lamp shade/mobile. Painted/natural wood peg/hook rail; wicker storage baskets.

A softly contrasting blue and yellow scheme creates a lively setting, without being overpowering.
The simple check theme for curtains, crib canopy, covers and pocket storage bag looks bright and cheerful.
A nursery motif border, color-coordinating dado and wallpaper add low-key pattern interest.
Brightly painted shelves with a display of favorite toys will catch the eye of a young baby.
Comfortable seating is important for you – for feeding, cuddling and reading bedtime stories.
Personalize a toy chest with a painted name and motif, and take the opportunity to add a cushioned seat top.

Merging the pretty with the practical is the key in this fresh yellow and green nursery. Thoughtful touches include the radiator cover – to protect small hands – woodstrip flooring and toning cupboard doors to hide clutter, as well as the jaunty fretwork shelf trims and simple slipcover on the chair.

Nursery Furnishings

The crib or cradle will take center stage in the nursery, so it is natural that all the furnishings should complement this. If you are using a pattern motif for curtains or a wallcovering, you can introduce this in some way – use a canopy rod to support a matching or coordinating fabric drape over the crib – or pick up the coloring through solids, checks or stripes for the crib set and blanket trims.

Choose an unfussy window treatment. Simple sill or full-length curtains can be draped back with holdbacks – perhaps with a novelty trim – or coordinating tiebacks. A roller blind to match is practical for controlling daytime shade, and can also feature a black-out backing if required.

If you can, place the changing pad on a surface at a suitable height for you – either a custom-made unit or the top of a chest or a work top with cupboards beneath. Keep all the necessary equipment and toiletries close at hand – in drawers, on a shelf above the mat or in roomy hanging fabric pockets and bags.

If you do not have a traditional nursing chair in the nursery, you can improvize by adding a slipcover to any low chair, or simply cover a deck chair in a color to suit the scheme. If space allows, team it with a small side table. As the baby grows, scaled down, child-height furniture will also be much appreciated; a small table and chair are both nursery basics, so try to incorporate these in the Soft Contemporary scheme.

Versatile features should always be a consideration in a nursery. Here, built-in cupboards provide a space for a changing pad and baby equipment, but can eventually hold toys and games.

Customize a simple crib with a pretty fabric drape, to match the crib set. Fresh spring green adds a bright color note here, in what would otherwise be a simple pastel scheme.

Looking light and airy, the simple curtain drapes and pretty pink setting flatter the traditionally dressed baby's cradle. A sturdy wooden crib in white or natural wood would look just as much at home here.

Ready and waiting for a toddler, child-size furniture is a sensible choice in an ever-changing nursery setting.

A comfortable nursing chair is a priority in any nursery. For a Soft Contemporary look, cover a traditional low-seated chair with a simple fabric design to blend in with the nursery color scheme.

97

STYLE DETAILS

One of the best parts of decorating a Soft Contemporary nursery is adding those special touches that personalize the room. If painting appeals to you, you can paint or stencil the baby's name on the end of the crib, or a toy chest, or design a simple frieze or mural of nursery figures. You could stitch a sampler picture or pillow, or make a patchwork quilt or appliqué picture to record special details.

Simple storage solutions are a priority, for clothes and accessories as well as toys. Baskets, boxes and bags are always popular in a nursery, so matching sets in different sizes and colors will look attractive and help to minimize any sense of clutter. A peg rail – at child and adult height – will help keep things tidy, and can hold wall pockets, clothes or toy bags.

Use versatile gingham checks as handy coordinates; choose them for accessories such as this diaper bag, in colors to complement the scheme.

A special changing table offers protective side rails and handy shelf space. Later on, it is a useful unit for toy storage.

Measuring height is a childhood fascination, so a charming painted growth chart, designed to coordinate with a border motif, will be a treasured memory of nursery days.

Rag baskets offer a new slant on the rag rug theme, and make ideal toy baskets. You can make them in fabrics to suit your nursery color scheme.

CHILDREN'S THEME ROOMS

Dramatic style rooms for children follow a theme; some highly individual decorative effects combined with practical ideas set the scene for a colorful world of fantasy and fun.

Once young children reach school age and become increasingly independent, their attentions turn to social interests and activities. Projects and collections, sports, hobbies and pets gradually find a place alongside their make-believe games and the fantasy worlds of early childhood. This is the time when Dramatic, boldly themed bedrooms are particularly popular, as both boys and girls welcome the opportunity to express their blossoming individuality in their surroundings.

Young children's color preferences are well defined, and so are their likes and dislikes. Although they have many interests in common, boys tend to focus on traditionally active interests, and girls develop their penchant for elaborate role-playing games. These directions are often reflected by their requests for room schemes. Settings for heroic adventures or fairytale princesses are all familiar and favorite decorative themes – but there are also some surprises.

▲ *With a stretch of the imagination, the family pet dog could be the inspiration for the unusual cornice in this child's room. The silhouette design has been decorated with bright splashes of primary color, so popular with young children, and chosen to coordinate with the rest of the room.*

▶ *Theme-linked accessories, such as this amusing dachshund peg rail, are the little details that help to create a particular style. Medium-density fiberboard (MDF) is an ideal material for this type of accessory.*

CHOOSING A THEME

Most children have lots of ideas about how they would like their bedroom to look, and, whether they share with a sibling or have a room to themselves, an arrangement to satisfy everyone can usually be found, however ambitious or fanciful the starting point.

Choose a theme that you can accommodate in a practical way, that will span a transitional period in a child's development, and is sufficiently flexible for you to replace details as interests gradually change. Before embarking on a theme, consider priorities such as room sharing with different age children and division of sleep and play space, as well as storage requirements. These are relevant at all stages, whatever the room size or theme, but they should influence your choice and are certain to provide useful pointers for an interesting decorative approach.

STYLE POINTERS

 THEMES **Action and adventure:** knights and castles, wild west, circus, sports, space travel, pre-history, nautical, tropics, wildlife.
Romantic: ballet, literary and media characters, countryside, day/night sky: rainbows, sun, moon and stars.

 WALLS **Patterns/plains:** hand-painted or paper collage murals, paint effects, stencils, stamped motifs, patterned wallpaper, borders, plain walls with patterned dado to complement the theme.
Architectural details: utilize alcoves/recesses for storage; screen them with roller blinds/theme doors.

 WINDOWS **Dress to complement:** create atmosphere with curtain or blind styles to suit the theme; novelty shaped cornices, decorated poles, tie/holdback details.

 FLOORING **Easy-care:** polished or painted boards, cork or vinyl tiles with rugs, plain wall-to-wall carpet.

 FABRICS **Patterns/solids/textures:** accentuate the theme with soft furnishings and bed linen in coordinated patterns and toning plains; cotton, calico, voile, appliqué designs.

 FURNITURE **Practical/adaptable/space saving:** decorate wardrobe, cupboard, chest of drawers to enhance the theme: create novelty frames/bed surrounds/headboards with MDF (medium-density fiberboard) cut to shape, or trompe l'oeil, fabric/wallpaper panels; decorate wood or metal, built-in or freestanding bed/bunks, under-bed storage, shelving, desk, chair, low table/trunk.

 LIGHTING **Practical/fun themes:** use dimmer switches for main light; practical desk/bedside light, character shades.

 ACCESSORIES **Storage/theme enhancers:** character headboard, noticeboard, wooden peg rails for clothes/toy bags, pillows, bean bags, stacking box/basket system, trunk/toy box, theater/play screen, bed drapes/mosquito nets; play bedspread, novelty clock, mirror.

Following a colorful check and daisy theme, pretty fabrics, romantic muslin drapes and a combination of clear bright colors create a versatile bedroom for a growing girl. Practical details include the charming window seat which provides valuable storage for toys and games, and the ruffle-trimmed protective cover on the bedside chest of drawers.

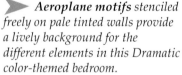 *Aeroplane motifs stenciled freely on pale tinted walls provide a lively background for the different elements in this Dramatic color-themed bedroom.*
A colorful rug, decorated with bold checks and stylized motifs, is the eye-catching inspiration for furniture and furnishings. Placed over plain toning carpet, the effect is spacious and comfortable.
Bold checks for curtains and bed linen look crisp and clean, and by echoing the border patterns and colors in the rug, help to create a well-balanced look.
Imaginatively painted furniture complements the lively color theme; vibrant turquoise, blue and yellow detailing show the molded panels to advantage.

A PRACTICAL APPROACH

Theme pitfalls to avoid, unless you are prepared to redecorate as soon as the fad is over, are those based on current crazes, such as the latest film or television character, or any theme likely to be dismissed as 'babyish' very quickly. In these instances the best compromise is to limit the favored subject to bed linen, wallpaper borders or accessories, which are easily changed, and take plain colors from the chosen design for the walls and other longer-lasting basics such as furniture and curtain fabrics.

Unless the theme is unashamedly romantic, calling for a bed with elaborate drapes or mosquito net, a bunk or platform bed with integral desk and shelving will free floor space for games. A lower bunk can double as a soft toy store or, draped with a customized cover, a hideaway den for creative play. In the well-ordered room below, which would appeal to a child who loves sports and games, ample storage space encourages tidiness. Aim to incorporate a desk and shelves for projects and school work; girls will also especially welcome a chest or surface with a mirror that can double as a dressing table.

Carpentry, artistic and sewing skills are a great bonus when creating a child's themed room, but you can compensate for any lack of these by providing a practical room layout, making bold use of color, and by encouraging children to contribute their own creative decorations. Most children enjoy drawing and collage (borders, panels and dados are ideal for this), and by making simple fabric designs with appliqué and fabric paints, you can decorate sheeting for curtains and accessories. Projects such as these can give your children a real sense of pleasure and achievement.

Here, a child's fascination for heavy vehicles is indulged with a dramatic mural. You could copy this eye-catching idea on a smaller scale, perhaps as a frieze using paint or paper collage.

Dynamic red, teamed with sturdy, functional furniture, emphasizes the sporty, active theme in this boy's room.

◀ *Block print motifs offer a quick way to complement a Dramatic theme. Teamed with an expanse of plain color, and printed on furniture or walls up to dado or picture rail height, they can be relied on to add lively interest in a bright and bold scheme.*

▲ *With a sweep of the curtains this child's bed becomes a private den or a theater stage. The built-in cupboard frame not only houses a standard bed and creative play space, but can be altered at a later date to accommodate changing needs.*

▶ *The dark wood furniture and the period-style, draped bed give this bedroom an exotic touch and a nostalgic charm. A jungle print wallpaper border and soft green parrot print bed linen point the way for a tropical adventure theme.*

▲ *On a tropical theme, any child would love a small table with legs shaped and painted to look like palm leaves.*

A zany fabric print featuring different hat styles inspires this quite extraordinary curtain holdback. You could adapt the idea to suit any theme.

THEME DETAILS

Adding the details to a child's themed bedroom is an activity to relish. You can effectively 'pull' a look together by finding accessories in the right colors and shapes to complement the theme, and by creating your own finishing touches.

▼ *Toy soldiers have enduring appeal, and this special guard would delight many young children. Panel doors create a window effect, which is ideal for this type of decorative approach.*

◄ A roll-up blind secured with contrast fabric ties offers a simple solution to unsightly clutter, as well as an ideal opportunity to use an attractive fabric to complement a theme.

▼ Motifs cut from wallcovering provide a great way to decorate a toy chest to match a room scheme. Finish with a coat of clear varnish to create a wipe-clean surface.

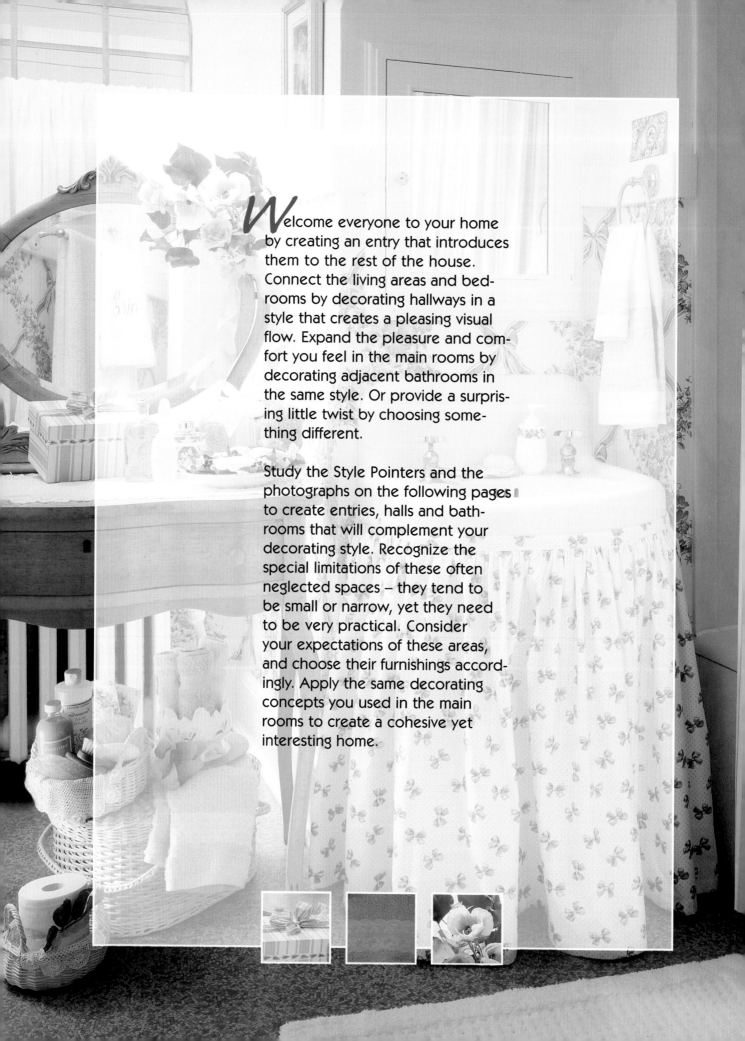

Welcome everyone to your home by creating an entry that introduces them to the rest of the house. Connect the living areas and bedrooms by decorating hallways in a style that creates a pleasing visual flow. Expand the pleasure and comfort you feel in the main rooms by decorating adjacent bathrooms in the same style. Or provide a surprising little twist by choosing something different.

Study the Style Pointers and the photographs on the following pages to create entries, halls and bathrooms that will complement your decorating style. Recognize the special limitations of these often neglected spaces – they tend to be small or narrow, yet they need to be very practical. Consider your expectations of these areas, and choose their furnishings accordingly. Apply the same decorating concepts you used in the main rooms to create a cohesive yet interesting home.

CLASSIC HALL

*Provide an impressive and inviting welcome to your home
with a Classic style entrance hall – traditionally furnished with
period accessories, it strikes a warmly familiar but elegant note.*

Your entrance hall acts as an introduction to your home, setting the tone for the rest of the house. A hall decorated and furnished in Classic style has a traditional look, but maximizes space and height with clear colors, imposing light fixtures and pale or shiny floors to create an airy, open feel. Period details are important and are easily added to a plain hall – corbels, ceiling moldings and cornices draw the eye upward, increasing the sense of height. Accessories also have a period feel, but are carefully chosen and placed – too much clutter will spoil the impact. A gilt-framed mirror scores on two counts, increasing the sense of light and space and adding a touch of grandeur; look for old candle sconces, china urns, imposing plant stands and other antique artifacts.

Pale colors and elegant furnishings set a formal period-style welcome in this Classic entrance area. The shiny finishes of gilt, glass and polished wood in the furnishings and accessories reflect the light back and forth, creating a spacious, airy feel.

107

CREATING THE STYLE

A Classic style hall, while impressive, should retain a sense of traditional good living and comfort. Pale colors from the warm side of the spectrum, such as creams, clear yellows and honey beige, make the most of the space. If you have a fairly spacious hall you can go for the more dramatic shades of peacock, rust or forest green, which make a rich backdrop for glittering candelabra and gilt. With dark colors, choose vinyl or gloss paint, or varnish over flat paint, to give a longer-lasting finish and a slight glaze.

STYLE POINTERS

 WALLS Light/glossy: sophisticated pale colors or rich shades with a gleaming finish; fancy paint finishes to imitate marble, stone or plasterwork; or softer effects such as colorwashing and ragging; stenciled borders.
Wallpapers: stripes, embossed or sculptured effects, formal classical or heraldic motifs, trompe l'oeil effect papers with stone block or marbled patterns; classical borders.

 WINDOWS Glass: decorative effects – stained, etched, sandblasted patterns.
Curtains and blinds: formal draperies, asymmetrically draped curtains on stairwell windows; London or Roman blinds, wooden slatted venetians.

 FLOORING Hard-wearing: polished wood, ceramic, stone- or marble-effect tiles; Plain or blended mid-tone color carpet.
Rugs: Turkish or Oriental rugs, flat weave or tufted traditional patterned runners.

 FABRICS Elegant: glossy chintzes, damasks, velvet, needlepoint.

 FURNITURE Period: polished woods, stone, wrought iron with glass.
Occasional pieces: console, half-moon and side tables; radiator covers with patterned grilles; small desks, chests and cupboards, hall stands; tall plant stands, grandfather clock, umbrella stand; occasional chairs in period styles.

 LIGHTING Imposing: chandeliers or glass lanterns; metal wall sconces; table lamps with metal or china bases; slender candle lamps with tiny shades.

 ACCESSORIES Graceful/decorative: gilt-framed mirror, pictures or prints in wood frames, symmetrically arranged; elegant vases with flowers or dried arrangements; stone or plaster figures.

Wallpapers with a touch of gold add extra sheen while broad, formal stripes have the correct period look and add height. Paint effects such as marbling, stone blocks or trompe l'oeil moldings hint at the grand homes of the past, and most of these effects are available in wallpaper.

Hard floors, such as wood, tiling, or vinyl sheeting, reflect the light, so adding to the feeling of spaciousness – and they are hard-wearing too. The diagonal lines of parquet flooring or traditional black-and-white tiles visually enlarge the floor space, pushing out the walls of a narrow hall. Carpet should be hard-wearing – berber or cord in plain or mottled beiges and grays are elegant and subtle.

◄ *Decorative paint effects in pale colors help open out restricted spaces.*
A gilt-framed mirror and glass chandelier increase the sense of light.
A radiator cover, painted to match the woodwork, looks attractive and provides a useful shelf.
Parquet flooring edged with a narrow black border looks suitably elegant and is typical of the Classic look.
Sophisticated accessories such as the turned wood candlesticks topped with small shades, and the lacquered umbrella stand, add a sharp contrast to the pale scheme.

▼ *Clear yellow makes a sunny background for the dried flower displays arranged at strategic points on this stairwell and lifts the darker tone of the practical carpet. The plain and delicate balusters are typical of the Classic look.*

CLASSIC STYLE FURNISHINGS

Most halls are restricted in terms of space, so choose your furniture to combine practicality and elegance. A radiator cover turns an ugly necessity into a useful shelf space in the narrowest hallway. If space allows, fit a small round table into a corner to take a lamp, vase of flowers and the telephone; look for one with a shelf or deep drawer beneath for directories. If your hall is wide enough, look for an elegant console table in glossy wood, or iron with a glass top. Or create your own table with a pair of stone urns topped with a sheet of glass. If floor space is limited you can achieve a table effect by mounting a glass or polished wood shelf on iron brackets or plaster corbels on the wall.

Create a formal arrangement on the table, setting a couple of small candlesticks on either side of a clock or piece of statuary, with pictures or a mirror formally arranged above. A table with one or more drawers is useful for keys, gloves and other clutter – a Classic hall needs to be kept tidy. If possible, coats and shoes should be tidied away in an understairs cupboard; a hall stand should be for effect only, or reserved for guests.

Again, if space allows, a single chair, or even a pair, is an ideal addition; look for period styles or graceful metal versions; upholstered seats or backs give the opportunity to add fabric color and texture. Alternatively, add an upholstered stool.

Clever paint effects give character and strong contrast to the plainest interior. The door and baseboard achieve the rich patina of polished wood, contrasting with the crisp white door frame. A shelf at dado height makes the most of limited space and creates a surface for flower arrangements. Classical prints above the shelf complete the elegant, Classic look.

◀ All the soft colors blended in this unusual scheme have been inspired by the rug that warms up the linoleum floor: rich red and blue glass in the door, slate blue paintwork, and the gentle rose pink and beige wall. The distinctive period effect balances the strong lines of the modern chair and chest, and harmonizes with the warm wood tones of the door frame and mirror frame.

Bends in the stairs will often accommodate a plant on a tall stand; if not, secure a decorative shelf or sconce to the wall for a dried-flower arrangement or trailing ivy.

Glowing light from chandeliers or glass lanterns, and gleaming gilt and brass are all part of the look. Wall sconces may continue the glow up the stairs, which should always be well lit for safety.

If you have a window in your entrance hall, it's likely to be fairly small, and heavy curtaining would be inappropriate; consider stained or etched glass panels to provide privacy without obscuring the window. Otherwise, add minimal curtaining or a blind, and/or simple drapery; a single curtain in a rich fabric, looped dramatically to one side, has a suitably grand effect. For a more restrained look, opt for a wooden slatted venetian blind, combined with a formal cornice or neat swags and tails.

◀ The delicate variations of fresh flowers and greenery, different woods, basketware, marble balls, and a gilded lamp with cream shade, blend gently with the gold and rust of paint and carpet – a restful combination.

▼ Rich red stair carpet and rugs enhance the sheen of the polished wood floor and newel post in this warm Classic entrance hall. A radiator cover creates a central feature for displaying wooden candlesticks and flowers, and leads the eye to the grandfather clock in the corner of the stairwell.

STYLE DETAILS

Choose door hardware carefully to complete the Classic look: scrolled, curving handles or knobs in ornate brass or sparkling glass give an elegant finish. Add brass or glass finger plates, and trim keys with swinging tassels. Choose decorative items very carefully – one large plaster bust has more impact than a clutch of smaller items. Hang pictures in pairs on either side of a mirror, or together in formal block arrangements, and group small ones down a picture ribbon topped with a bow beside a door.

▶ *A few aged items add distinctive character to the Classic style. Look for antique textiles to drape over tables; old and worn terra-cotta bottles and bowls blend beautifully with seed heads or dried flowers; and tinted varnish rubbed into stark white plaster busts gives an impressive, timeworn appearance.*

▶ *The reddish gleam of a bronze-colored candle sconce backed by a glittering mirror makes a striking contrast to the deep blue wall.*

▼ *Rich textures are set against an equally rich color in this carefully matched grouping. A peacock blue wall makes a glowing backdrop for tiny detailed bird pictures grouped on an ornate tapestry band; a small Oriental lamp set on a pretty polished table has a striking black pleated shade; a cherry-colored woven throw further enriches a detailed chair back.*

◀ *Achieving a sense of harmony with a pleasing balance of textures and shapes is an important consideration in the Classic hall. The elegant lines of a Hepplewhite-style chair are shown to advantage in this formal grouping.*

COUNTRY COTTAGE HALL

*The proportions of the Country Cottage hall vary from home
to home – in some homes it may be just a little corridor, while in others
the front door may open directly into a welcoming room.*

Whatever its size, the Country Cottage hall is an accommodating place, where charming, homey furnishings and accessories invariably jostle for wall and floor space alongside the coats and jackets, hats and scarves, and the equipment of outdoor pursuits such as boots and walking sticks.

Since country cottages come in many guises, from small terrace properties to dream homes with exposed beams and multiple levels, there are subtle shifts in decorative influence and detail. What all Country Cottage halls have in common, though, is a feeling for a rural setting – a promise of simple comforts and an atmosphere that looks 'lived in' and is quietly in tune with the changing seasons. If you yearn for a breath of country air in your home, you can take many elements from the Country Cottage hall and adapt them to an urban setting – especially since cozy proportions are a feature of many older homes. For larger halls in urban homes you can use country colors, fabric prints and accessories to capture some of the typical style elements.

▷ *Whether or not you live in the countryside, a hallway with rural green paintwork and simple wood paneling will suggest a country atmosphere. Develop the nostalgic theme with pretty floral curtains and a collection of handcrafted accessories such as a painted umbrella stand, animal cutouts and some charmingly rustic picture frames (inset).*

CREATING THE STYLE

In many country cottages, especially where the front door opens directly into a living room, a small anteroom, or a side or back entrance to the property, can be used as a functional hall area for everyday comings and goings. In these service areas, which often lead to a larger, more comfortable living room-cum-hall, the accent is on practicalities – a quarry-tiled floor, sturdy doormats, storage shelves, coat hooks, a muddy boot rack – and the trappings of rural life. In the main hall area, where the staircase and rooms lead off, the decor will have a more comfortable, mellow look, with cozy soft furnishings and decorative displays.

A typical cottage has small windows, so walls are traditionally painted in a pale color to compensate for any lack of light. A pastel color-wash, or discreetly sprigged floral pattern above half-paneled walls will help counterbalance any gloomy corners. Alternatively, create a cozy effect with a rich but muted plain color. A contrast between dark and light is very much a country cottage feature – especially in a period property where shafts of light play on dark beams and cast shadows from low ceilings – so create this atmosphere with woodwork in a dark, matte or satin paint finish or to contrast with the walls.

STYLE POINTERS

 WALLS Pale/rich: rough-textured plaster with warm-toned, light colorwash or rich plain color; sprig or floral wallcovering; natural wood tone or dark painted paneling and woodwork.

 WINDOWS Curtains: simple gathered or cased styles on curtain poles; frilled valance or covered cornice; matching/cord tiebacks.

 FLOORING Rustic tiles/boards: quarry tiles, flagstone effects; stained/polished floorboards.
Rugs: Oriental carpet/runner; coir/sisal/coconut matting; plain/mottled stair carpet.

 FABRICS Pretty/rich muted: cotton and chintz sprigs, florals, checks and stripes; plain and floral linen; lace; velvets; crewel embroidery and needlepoint for upholstery.

 FURNITURE Period/rustic: simple, period-style dark oak/pine chest or bench; polished wood gateleg/pedestal table; spindle-back/period chair with rush/cushion seat; wing armchair; hall stand; modern alternatives in wicker/cane.

 LIGHTING Cozy: candle wall fixtures with tailored fabric lamp shades; hanging lantern/oil lamp; period-style table lamp with floral print fabric shade.

 ACCESSORIES Heirloom/collectibles: grandfather or pendulum wall clock; barometer; wood/ornate iron umbrella stand; wood/gilt-framed mirror; antique prints/maps; glass case specimens, period china; fresh/dried country flower/plant displays; wicker/copper/brass/pewter containers; iron doorstop; bootscraper.

▲ *When the front door opens directly into a living room, the accent is on comfort and practicality. A warm and welcoming color scheme, cozy soft furnishings and a traditional quarry-tiled floor are typical features of Country Cottage style.*

▶ *A practical, tiled entrance leads into a comfortably furnished reception area.*
Pale walls create a feeling of light and space in a naturally dark area.
The grandfather clock and attractive dark wood furniture add authentic period charm.
Cottage garden flowers add a fresh, summer accent.
Traditional floral print covers protect a comfortable armchair.
A collection of period-style prints add to the welcoming atmosphere.

HALL FURNISHINGS

Although a Country Cottage hall often looks delightfully 'busy', space is at a premium, so simplicity is the key for furniture and furnishings. One or two pieces take pride of place, and these could include a well-polished wooden chest, table or bench, a prized grandfather clock or period-style coatrack. A hall table or chest also provides an ideal surface for a seasonal flower or plant display, as well as for gleaming brass, copper or pewter ware, and for a pretty china, glass or country pottery collection.

Save splashes of pattern and color for neat, sill-length curtains – prettily caught up with cords and tiebacks – or for a heavy door curtain, for covers on chairs and pillows, or in a traditional, patterned rug.

Create the slightly cramped but cozy feeling of typical low ceilings and odd-angled wall shapes with a closely grouped collection of antique-style prints and pictures, or a wall-mounted display of country-ware and china plates, and continue the theme up the stairs. Candle wall lights with colored fabric shades, or period-style sconces will cast a warm and subtle glow, and help contribute to a nostalgic, bygone atmosphere.

▲ *An appreciation of simple, homey things is strikingly evident in this lovingly cared for hall. Glossy paint, a well-buffed stone floor and a polished wood table, topped with a verdant fern, all celebrate the timeless qualities of Country Cottage style.*

▶ *With a few well-chosen accessories, you can create a Country Cottage look in any hall. A pine console table, a rustic umbrella stand complete with character walking sticks, and a display of grasses in a shiny copper pot, help set the scene.*

◀ In this plain-and-simple, country-style hall, an exuberant display of colorful garden flowers reflects the time of year in a delightfully dramatic way. Woven wicker furniture and honey-toned flooring and accessories add to the mellow atmosphere.

▲ The soft tones of stripped pine and the warm earth pigments of the walls immediately conjure up a Country Cottage atmosphere. They also work perfectly as a backdrop for well-loved period pieces in the hall, such as a small pedestal table and a collection of gilt-framed pictures.

▶ Strong contrasts between dark and light and old and new are a familiar cottage-style theme. Here, period beams, dark wood furniture and traditional framed prints are set against white walls and a streamlined staircase.

STYLE DETAILS

Little touches to delight the eye in the Country Cottage hall are relatively easy to collect. Rustic accessories include basketware and simple wooden boxes or frames that you can embellish with country-craft details. Dried seed and flower collages, pressed leaves and stenciled trims all make beautiful displays to complement the seasons. You can start a collection of curiously carved walking sticks, an amusing choice of country hats, or other witty themes with country links. These could include weather-beaten flowerpots and containers or small antique farming or dairy implements.

Set on a window ledge or hall table, a basket of seasonal country fruit – either real or everlasting – will add a cottage-style finishing touch to your decorations.

For country lovers in town, use a picket fence box to hold keys, gloves or the mail – the bits and pieces that collect on every hall table – as a daily reminder of rustic pleasures farther afield.

Polished wood, gleaming glass and cabbage rose prints all contribute to the comfortable look that sums up Country Cottage style. Rich colors contrast well with mellow wood and glinting metal accents.

A sturdy garden bench will add an appropriately rustic note to any would-be cottage hallway. Here, a wax-resist stencil design of trailing ivy leaves highlights a simple country look.

CLASSIC BATHROOM

Enjoying the fruits of traditional design, the Classic style bathroom is discreetly luxurious, with generously proportioned fixtures, quality materials and elegant furnishings.

◄ *The look is elegant yet understated in this pure white scheme, where texture – particularly in the attractive trellis panels, wall paneling and marble surrounds – provides low-key pattern interest. Smart, period-style fixtures such as the chrome and porcelain shower system (below) are typical features in a Classic bathroom.*

Attention to detail and a love of traditional workmanship are very much in evidence in the Classic style bathroom, where the atmosphere is reassuringly sumptuous without being showy. A handsome period-style bath and accommodating washbasin in pristine white take pride of place against an elegant, uncluttered background. Luxurious marble, rich, dark wood or painted paneling feature prominently in many schemes, while soft, clear color, smart, tailored furnishings and fresh-looking fabrics complement smooth, hard surfaces.

CREATING THE STYLE

Whatever its size or shape, the Classic bathroom has a well-defined sense of space. The look is either pale, with light-colored walls, plain tiles or smooth marble effects, or is planned around a strong, muted color scheme – often based on a rich, "Historic" paint shade.

Choose a traditional white bathroom set with good quality chrome or gold finish faucets. If space permits, make the tub a focal point – perhaps on a raised block, or placed centrally in the room. Set it in a marble or tile-width surround, with elegant dark stained wood, or hand-painted medium-density fiberboard (MDF) side panels. The sink should match these grand proportions – either as a large pedestal style, or a good-size basin set into a marble or glass-topped vanity cupboard with paneled doors. For a small bathroom, simply scale down the effect, but retain these key features.

For a custom-made look – unless you have a chunky period-style radiator – fit radiator covers with trellis or metal grille panels, and paint them to blend with the color scheme. The top shelf provides a useful display surface.

The bathroom flooring should help to define the space – black-and-white checkered effects are traditional, as are marble effects or linoleum with inlay borders – either in black and white or a blend of stone-colored neutrals. Otherwise choose a plain, neutral color flooring, or sealed boards or wood blocks and Oriental rugs.

▶ *This period-style bathroom set in soft white looks elegant with its rope-twist edging.*
Colorwashed wood paneling in an antiqued finish has an essentially Classic style quality.
Black-and-white checkered floor tiles are timeless and practical.
Classical portrait studies in gilt frames underline this sophisticated style.
Period-look furniture and furnishings have an understated elegance.

STYLE POINTERS

 WALLS Pale/tiled: mid-tone flat paint; wallcoverings with discreet patterns, narrow stripes; traditional plain white tiles, contrast color borders; marble/marble effects.

 WINDOWS Formal: tailored, lined curtains with cornice or swags; tiebacks/tassels; brass or dark wood curtain poles.
Blinds: ruched Austrian; pleated London blind; shaped hem roller blind.

 FABRICS Traditional/elegant: glazed chintz florals/stripes; stylized period-style prints.

 FLOORING Marble/black and white: elegant marble slabs; formal checkered tiles; traditional wood-block styles.
Rugs: period/traditional wool rug; plain cotton mats.

 BATHROOM FIXTURES Period-style/white: simple, chunky lines, retro-style set; roll-top bath; traditional chrome/gold finish fittings – taps, bath basket, wall-mounted soap holders, chunky towel rail; clean-lined, clear glass shower panel; toilet with discreet/paneled-in, or high-level tank; retro-style radiator or fitted radiator cover with metal/trellis grille.

 FURNITURE Finely crafted/period: mahogany/dark wood effect/hand-painted or marble bath panels, matching cupboards or custom-made built-in units; period-style table/chest of drawers; wooden/painted cane chair or upholstered small chair.

 LIGHTING Period style/elegant: brass/chrome and glass dome ceiling fixture; glass/turned wood/metal wall lights.

 ACCESSORIES Elegant/traditional: luxurious plain towels; wood paneled laundry box; slatted boardwalk/cork bathmat or plain cotton tufted mats; sea sponge; gilt/dark wood or white-painted mirror frame; gilt/black- framed studies of classical architecture, antique fashion plates or landscapes; antique-style porcelain/glass containers; classical busts/urns.

◀ *This elegant bathroom may be spacious, but you can capture the same skilful blend of dark and light contrasts in any size room. Here, rich wood tones and an elegantly pale setting are complemented by gleaming gold accents in typical Classic style.*

CLASSIC STYLE FURNISHINGS

Although the Classic bathroom is designed as a formal and rather gracious place, practical needs are comfortably arranged and well considered. Bathroom clutter is stored behind elegantly paneled doors, so that details of outstanding merit, such as a gilt mirror, a classical urn or a collection of period-style prints or pretty glass containers, can be fully appreciated. This makes good sense, since besides promoting a feeling of space, Classic style furnishings are attractive in their own right.

The Classic window treatment – whether full-length curtains, a valance or cornice – should be a slightly relaxed version of a formal style. The fabrics may be lavishly trimmed, but must also be practical – you can always team an elaborately draped curtain pole or swagged valance with

▶ *Pale buttercream has a warm, unifying effect, and is a favourite color choice for Classic style schemes. Used for walls and built-in units, it harmonizes well with the subtle shades of the creamy marble surrounds and trims, and complements the floral chintz curtains.*

◀ *In this Classic bathroom, a custom-made cover discreetly screens the water tank, and makes a decorative feature. The marble-effect paneling adds a Classic style note, as does the traditional chair and the pretty toile de Jouy-style curtains.*

▶ *A custom-made built-in bathroom utilizes space efficiently, freeing surfaces for decorative features and creating a chance to focus on soft furnishings. Here, the silk-wrapped curtain pole and trimmed curtains add a contrast color note and, in true Classic style, look elegant and understated.*

a toning pull-up blind for privacy. Traditional stripes, period-style floral and figurative chintzes, watered silks or heavy lace are all suitable fabrics. As trimmings, fringed edgings, tassel tiebacks or gilt holdbacks look elegant and are in keeping with the style. A decorative shower curtain may also match the window treatment, but should always be lined with a standard, plain shower-proof curtain.

Wall lights are often more atmospheric than ceiling lights, and in the Classic bathroom these can be a strong feature – perhaps teamed with discreetly recessed ceiling spotlights. Look for antiqued candle sconce or torch styles, period-style glass shades and adjustable arm lights with pleated fabric shades. For a central light, choose a traditional glass and metal dome or pendant bowl fixture and wall switches, to comply with bathroom safety regulations.

◢ *In a scheme inspired by the classical themes of Wedgwood blue and white decorations, the accent is on creating a luxurious atmosphere. Teamed lavishly with black marble, this bathroom aims for a grand effect.*

◀ *Yellow with black and white is an enduring Classic theme, with overtones of the elegant Georgian period. All the elements here are finely balanced to complement one another, from the imposing architectural print above the spendid black marble-topped tub, to the swagged window blind over the period-style radiator.*

CLASSIC DETAILS

While keeping the scheme simple, try to include a pretty period-style table, wall cabinet or shelf in the bathroom to display Classic style accessories. These can include bath salts and oils in period-style porcelain or glass bottles and containers. Turned wood, tortoiseshell-, ebony- and ivory-effect boxes and bristle brushes are also appropriate. Copies of classical studies – sculptures, urns, figure drawings and friezes – are very much in style, as are graceful specimen plants. Introduce an orchid or fern in a cachepot, or create an elegant flower arrangement. On a practical note, add a traditional cane-seated upright chair, or a little upholstered nursing chair – to match the curtains.

◄ *The smallest details can give big clues about a certain style, so choose traditional, real bristle brushes to complement a Classic style bathroom.*

▲ *As a symbol of the style, a classical urn makes an impressive repository for towels and creates a bold textural accent in this pristine white bathroom.*

▲ *Traditional bathroom fixtures should have the time-honored hallmarks of quality craftsmanship. An ornate backplate and muted gold finish make this stylish soap holder a perfect choice.*

◄ *The accessories in a master bathroom usually follow the style of the adjoining room. These lamp shades complement the soft, warm color scheme and are entirely in keeping with both a Classic style bathroom and bedroom.*

SOFT CONTEMPORARY BATHROOM

*Comfortable good looks, a practical layout and efficient design
details underline the Soft Contemporary bathroom. Surfaces are
streamlined, textures are decorative and clutter is under control.*

One of the most appealing characteristics of the Soft Contemporary bathroom is a feeling of light and space. This is created with a subtle color scheme based on pale and mid tones, light-colored woods and the fluid, clean lines of the fixtures and unfussy furnishings.

Whatever the size of the bathroom – whether it is a busy family room or has only one user – the look is uncluttered. Sensible and good-looking storage ideas include built-in cupboards, drawers, shelves, baskets and bags, which help to concentrate the eye on the main features – an elegant but low-key bathroom set, smart and simple soft furnishings and attractive, modern accessories.

▲ The softly curving lines of the bathroom set are typical of Soft Contemporary style, where updated classic shapes look elegant and understated. A quiet color scheme of aqua, white and chrome, and smart but simple accessories such as these on the left, with their contrasting gold tones, complement the practical, comfortable look.

CREATING THE STYLE

As the center of attention, Soft Contemporary bathroom fixtures look smart in typical white, soft cream or palest gray. The shapes are sculptural and rounded, with pleasing proportions that hint at influences from more traditional styles. Organizing space in the bathroom is a priority, so after considering the placement of the fixtures, creating a streamlined effect is high on the agenda.

Color plays an important role here, as you can use it to camouflage or integrate different features. Pipes can be boxed in – perhaps with panels up to dado height – and designed to incorporate storage space, to help eliminate clutter. When decorated in the same color as the walls above, the effect is neat and clean-lined. A paneled dado with built-in cupboards and shelves also provides a useful top ledge for accessories and towels. Similarly, an integrated sink and vanity unit, or cupboards that continue or echo the lines of the panels, also help to create a spacious effect.

Feeling warm and comfortable is important in any bathroom. In the Soft Contemporary style, pale but warm-toned woods and paint colors and subtle textures help you achieve this. A hint of warming pink or yellow in the white of an all-white scheme will take the chill off a cold room, and create a spacious look in a small or dark bathroom. Spice colors, warm earth tones, and calming, muted blues and greens also look mellow and cozy tempered with warm creams and honeyed wood finishes.

Underfoot, warm-to-the-touch and practical woodstrip-effect flooring (choose this rather than real wood, which may not tolerate damp conditions), looks authentic and provides a sleek, Contemporary style surface. Choose from the light tones of ash, limed pine or beech. A wood-color flooring also creates a balance for fashionable pale wood furniture and bathroom accessories. As an alternative to a wood-effect floor, choose pale-colored, plain ceramic tiles, or a specialized bathroom carpet in a neutral shade.

STYLE POINTERS

 WALLS Pale/understated: paint in flat colors – light/mid-tone pastels; broken-color paint effects such as sponging, stippling, colorwashing; limed/painted tongue-and-groove/flat paneled dado.
Wallcoverings: faux paint effects; subtle checks, stripes, low-key pattern motifs.
Tiles: plain white/cream, pale/mid-tone or delicately mottled/patterned.

 WINDOWS Curtains: simple, informal versions of traditional styles; cotton and voile; solids, checks, stripes, theme motifs; gathered and tab styles on rods or poles, valance headings.
Blinds/shutters: Roman, pleated, roller styles, wooden-slatted venetians, plantation shutters.

 FLOORING Light/natural: pale wood-strip effect; white/cream, plain/mottled ceramic tiles; stone effects; plain/semi-plain linoleum/vinyl; neutral color bathroom carpet.
Rugs: short pile/woven cotton mat; wood slat bath mat.

 BATHROOM FIXTURES Fluid lines/unfussy: simple sculpted shapes in white ceramic or soft, pale color; self-color, pale wood or tiled bath panels; clean-lined shower panels.
Hardware: chrome/gold finish/ceramic fixtures; updated classic faucet shapes or streamlined lever styles; coordinating towel rails, toilet roll/toothbrush/soap holders; glass or color-matched shelves; covered radiators, or smart, built-in towel rails.

 FURNITURE Pale wood/metal: built-in vanity units/cupboards in smooth maple/beech, limed pine or painted wood, with marble, granite, light wood or tiled tops; Contemporary style metal and plywood chairs/tables and wicker styles.

 LIGHTING Streamlined/soft: recessed ceiling halogen spots; glass bowl central fixture; plaster/chrome/brass sconces; updated period styles.

 ACCESSORIES Simple/modern: plain mirror or with feature frame in painted/distressed/pale wood; shaped shelf edge trims; plain white, pale or color accent towels; novelty print shower curtains; bright pastel plastics; roomy laundry basket/bin; framed art prints; fresh flowers; scented candles; colored glass bottles; collectors' shells.

In a pale, warm color scheme, where the walls and floor share similar tones, streamlined built-in units add to the illusion of space. The bathroom fixtures are curvy and modern and a simple window blind highlights the terra-cotta color accents.

▲ *A calming aquamarine color scheme* used throughout creates a pleasing sense of space and order.

The gently curved lines of the pale colored bathroom fixtures are typical of the elegant and understated Soft Contemporary style.

Natural wood-effect flooring flatters the uncluttered Contemporary scheme with its clean lines and soft, warm tones.

A simple cotton rug adds a vital color and pattern accent to the bathroom.

Pictures and accessories are low-key, but express a sense of individual style.

Wooden shutters look smart and modern, painted white to complement the Soft Contemporary scheme.

BATHROOM FURNISHINGS

The hallmarks of Soft Contemporary style are simplicity and comfort, where curving shapes and soft textures take precedence over more angular Contemporary looks.

Window treatments are practical and functional without being stark, with soft lines and subtle detailing that flatter their surroundings, but are never fussy. This understated look is created using natural materials and fabrics – either toning solids and neutrals, and often, checks and stripes. Curtains may have simple gathered or tab headings, or hang as panels, held with decorative clips from rods or poles. Wooden-slatted blinds and shutters also suit the style, and are a good foil for any other wood tones in the room. Both fabrics and wood finishes strike a good textural balance with hard, shiny surfaces such as ceramic tiles, enamel, porcelain and chrome fixtures.

Faucets and shower hardware are streamlined and sleek in a chrome or gold finish, or combined with ceramic to color-match the fixtures, but they retain more traditional design features than ultra-modern styles. Shower panels are plain rather than embellished, with simple stripes or minimal surface decoration. Shower curtains can provide a splash of color or a focal point design in an otherwise low-key scheme; alternatively, they are solid to match the fixtures or tiles.

Countertops may be tiled, in a pale wood finish to blend with flooring, or a light color granite or marble. Or they may be painted to match the rest of the scheme, and topped with a protective layer of glass that also adds a stylish note.

▲ *Patterns and textures are carefully balanced to create a coordinated look in this soft taupe and pale mauve bathroom. The lightness of the color scheme helps to blend the various elements such as the check walls, floral fabrics and the eye-catching decorative molding trim.*

◄ *In a family bathroom, jaunty blue and yellow stripes and checks complement a nautical theme in a low-key scheme. Built-in units incorporate shelves and cupboards, to keep clutter to a minimum – an essential feature of the style.*

➤ *Comfortable and practical, homey little touches in this Soft Contemporary bathroom include pictures and collectibles to complement a gentle blue and mellow wood tone color scheme.*

▼ *The smooth, sculptural qualities of Soft Contemporary bathroom fixtures are shown to advantage here against a glowing spicy red background. An expanse of warm white and the mellow wood floor, furniture and accessories combine to create a pleasing visual balance.*

Style Details

In a plain and simple scheme, towels can be relied on to introduce accent color or maintain a good tonal balance. Use accents carefully to prevent the color from jumping around – in the Soft Contemporary bathroom, the effects can be vibrant, but are subtle and low-key rather than bold. A patterned rug can also provide a vital focal point. Stripes and simple patterns have a freshness that suits the Soft Contemporary style and, in inexpensive cotton weaves, they are practical too.

In a scheme based on neutrals and naturals, a slatted ramin wood bathmat adds textural interest. Its blond tones blend well with a natural wood mirror or picture frame, and balance with a folding calico laundry bag or pale wicker basket.

Dark metallic accents also add interesting shade and texture. A curvy iron curtain rod, chair or stool, or a focal point mirror frame can add interesting texture, as well as an individual touch.

▲ When space is at a premium, stylishly simple solutions to storing clutter are essential. Here, drawstring bags in ticking stripes, and black-and-white striped boxes lend a charming graphic quality to an all-white scheme.

▲ A practical calico laundry hamper folds away neatly to transport the contents to the washing machine, and has the right kind of simple good looks necessary to make it a key accessory in a Soft Contemporary bathroom.

➤ Cotton twist bath mats provide the perfect way to add color accents to the bathroom. Available in a choice of bright but subtle colors and white, there should be one to flatter your scheme.

COUNTRY COTTAGE BATHROOM

*This nostalgic style combines traditional looks with modern comforts;
period bathroom fixtures, charming fabrics and accessories combine
to create a relaxing, stress-free atmosphere.*

▲ *Essential elements of the
Country Cottage
bathroom are a fresh color scheme
and mellow period details. Here, a pretty
sprig-print sink skirt adds a charming
touch to this feminine scheme. Color-
coordinated accessories in pink and
green (inset) add the delicate finishing
touches typical of this style.*

The essence of Country Cottage style is simplicity – an original cottage bathroom would have been very basic indeed. The modern interpretation rejects the discomfort and concentrates on re-creating rustic charm and period detail with aging paint finishes and effects, pretty fabrics and old-fashioned accessories. You may not have a bathroom with beams or other authentic cottage features – a sloping ceiling, odd angles or lattice windows are a plus – but any small bathroom, especially one with white bathroom fixtures, offers a promising start. A cozy atmosphere is central to the style and a small bathroom is perfect for creating this feel. The look is also reasonably easy and inexpensive to create.

CREATING THE STYLE

Country style is essentially practical, never fussy or overdone. Victorian fixtures are perfect in the Country Cottage bathroom, but you can blend modern or colored fixtures into the scheme by choosing a patterned wallcovering or fabric print in toning colors. You might also change modern faucets to a traditional cross-head style, replace acrylic bath panels with wood paneling, or dress an unsuitable sink with a fabric skirt.

The bathroom walls are a good starting point for creating the style. Capture the look with tiles or tongue-and-groove paneling up to dado height; tiles may be white or a pale color, possibly with a small floral motif. Restrict full height tiles to a shower area, to avoid a clinical look. Decorate above the dado with a pale colorwash, or use a mini-floral wallcovering. You can extend this over the ceiling to "lower" it, or to integrate any sloping angles.

For the floor, aim for a natural look with wood finishes or rustic terra-cotta tiles, or replace these with cork or vinyl tiles and soft rag rugs or cotton mats.

Light the bathroom with a small central fixture or simple wall sconces, with a period fluted glass shade or frosted bowl and antiqued metal finish.

> *Pale walls, honey pine woodwork and a pretty window treatment are key features in a Country Cottage bathroom. A decorative border of colorful tiles around the tub and a lacy shower curtain add period-style details.*

STYLE POINTERS

 WALLS Pale/rough plaster: white/muted or colorwashed walls; stamp or stencil motifs; small floral wallpaper; dado with stripped or painted tongue-and-groove paneling.
Wall tiles: to dado height; white with period-style border tiles; Delft blue or Victorian flower tiles, mini flower sprig.

 WINDOWS Small: lattice panes or deep windowsills are special features.
Curtains: pretty but unfussy; simple cased or gathered styles; floral prints/sprigs/stripes and checks; frilled valances/café or lace curtains.
Blinds: simple styles with pretty fabric valance or patterned roller blind/matching curtains.

 FLOORS Rustic: stripped or painted wood; quarry tiles; natural fiber floorcovering; cork/vinyl tiles; wooden slatted bath mats; soft braided or hooked rag rugs for warmth.

 BATHROOM FIXTURES Period: White porcelain sink; freestanding bath or paneled in pine/dark wood; antique-style brass or chrome faucets/bath basket/shower fixtures; porcelain toilet with high-level tank.

 FURNITURE Period: simple painted or stripped pine table, chest, chair with cane seat or pretty cushion; rustic pine or white/pale painted wooden shelves.

 LIGHTING: Simple: traditional lights/simple sconces in metal or opaque glass; hanging light with period-style fluted glass shade.

 ACCESSORIES Period/collectables: antique glass; flower-sprigged ceramics; old-fashioned prints with distressed metal or wood frames; jugs of wild flowers; bowls of potpourri; baskets; lace-trimmed towels; ceramic/brass doorknob.

▼ *Tongue-and-groove paneling*, painted in a traditional flat buff color, and softly toning walls create a restful background for pretty fixtures and accessories.

Period-style white bathroom fixtures, brass faucets and a high water tank are hallmarks of the Country Cottage look.

Floral fabric for cased curtains and folding blinds has a nostalgic, country-fresh look.

Stripped floorboards are very much in style, and the soft rag rug adds a cottage-craft detail.

A rustic wooden chair and stool, antique china and colorful glass accessories all evoke Country Cottage style.

BATHROOM FURNISHINGS

Windows and walls are the natural focus for any pattern detail. Patterns should be soft and fresh; small florals and mini-print cottons, and chintz with coordinating wallcoverings, or checks and narrow stripes are all in style. Cottage-style window treatments are essentially simple, but they offer a perfect chance to introduce pattern and texture, or soften an otherwise plain scheme. Lacy drapes, prettily frilled valances and tieback details all enhance the style. You can also recycle pretty embroidered linens and antique lace borders, using them to make window blinds or drapes, and trims for towels and basket linings.

If space allows, include a small pine chest of drawers, or a table or linen basket in wicker or bamboo. These provide useful storage and are perfect for displaying Country Cottage accessories. A simple stripped or painted wooden chair with a rush or cane seat is pretty and practical, and gives you the chance to make a cushion to coordinate with curtains or walls. With all cottage-style furnishings think simple, pretty and practical.

Simplicity is the keynote in this soft, creamy scheme. The charming window treatment has all the freshness of cottage style and adds an elegant flourish to this otherwise understated look.

A large recessed window is a good-looking feature in any room. Here, a window seat, pretty curtains and lots of plump pillows make the most of this detail. The cozy, comfortable look is backed up by mellow pine paneling and a warm, color-coordinated design for walls and fabrics.

No Country Cottage bathroom is complete without old ceramic jugs and jars, glass bottles, natural wood and lace-trimmed accessories.

A floral wallcovering and soft color paint effects, combined with pretty accessories in toning colors, create an "old world" atmosphere.

A tall and handsome pine pedestal and old-fashioned towel rail are traditional touches in this cottage bathroom. Sprig-patterned tiles, lacy sheers and pretty stencil motifs complete the period look.

135

STYLE DETAILS

Choosing accessories for the Country Cottage bathroom is a perfect excuse to indulge in a little nostalgia and a love of period detail. Lace-trimmed linens and towels, Victorian china collectibles and prints; wash bowls and pitchers, pretty glass bottles, baskets with scented soaps or fragrant potpourri or a simple jug of country flowers set on mellow pine shelves all evoke fond thoughts of the past and a quieter way of life.

▲ *Romantic and feminine – fresh flowers, fragrant bath oils in gleaming cut glass, prettily packaged soaps, potpourri and lace-trimmed towels – all are delightfully luxurious additions to the nostalgic style.*

▲ *A floral print and cheerful checks add colorful notes to a plain window. A jug of fresh flowers and the pretty china collection complete the theme.*

▼ *Old-style bath accessories made from natural materials contribute a special period charm.*

▲ *On a whimsical note, a weathered picket fence storage box and basket nest of soaps are amusing rustic additions to a Country Cottage bathroom.*

DRAMATIC BATHROOM

A Dramatic bathroom is an indulgent haven for those with a passion for ambience and theatrical flair. It appeals to the senses with enticing colors, glorious fabrics and fabulous fixtures.

When you enter a Dramatic bathroom you leave mundane cares behind. Escapism is the inspiration, whether the look you aspire to is soft and romantic, exotic and mysterious or just dramatically different. Creating a special setting with a sense of theater is paramount, with a dramatic focal point, eye-catching details or a bold use of color and pattern.

Because Dramatic style exudes theatricality, it follows that the decorations in your bathroom may owe more to effect than substance, so a stylish flourish need not be prohibitively expensive. Think about working with beautiful elements – serene, harmonious colors or colorful contrasts, richly patterned fabrics and coordinates, sensual shapes and textures – putting these looks together calls for more dash than cash. Whatever your theme, just make sure that window and wall treatments, floor surfaces, and accessories all contribute in some way to achieving your chosen effect.

The heavenly blue color scheme and the golden sun, moon and star motifs suggest that celestial influences are at work here, creating an atmospheric setting for serious relaxation. The roll-top bath with its period-style fixtures plays a starring role in the drama – supported by the sumptuously draped curtains and gleaming accessories. Soft candlelight and fragrant oils would add further mystery to this romantic theme.

137

CREATING THE STYLE

The dramatic bathroom is for lingering in, so it is important to create a warm, inviting atmosphere. You can achieve this with color, good heating and soft-toned adjustable lighting.

The bath itself may take pride of place as a focal point. A freestanding bath can be in flamboyant period style – perhaps with impressive drapes and coronet – or positioned with elegant simplicity in a dramatically minimalist setting. If the fixtures in your bathroom are less grand, concentrate on color, texture, fabrics and wallcoverings to create a sense of drama. You can fit a canopy over a freestanding or built-in bath, install an extravagant window treatment and hang a remarkable mirror in most size bathrooms, or decorate with a range of flamboyant coordinates and accessories, to transform the space into an inspiring retreat.

Painted murals and trompe l'oeil effects are two decorative treatments that are entirely in place in the Dramatic bathroom. These can range from space-altering fantasy effects to a clever disguise for an unwanted feature.

A lavender and lime color scheme combines fresh, modern looks with sophisticated period style.

Antique bath and fixtures *hint at a love of classic elegance.*

Luxurious drapes strike a dramatic note *over the bath – and ensure its place as a glorious focal point.*

Ornate gilt wall ornaments *make a flamboyant style statement, and create a visual link with other Midas-touch accessories.*

Cool French limestone *covers the floor with a satin-smooth sheen, adding to the air of refined sophistication.*

STYLE POINTERS

 WALLS Eye-catching: bold in matte or shiny finish; paint effects; murals; dados, wood paneling; marble. Period-style patterns.
Wall tiles: Victorian style with embossed motifs; strong, glossy colored solids.

 WINDOWS Flamboyant: sumptuous fabrics/bold colors or fine textiles; decorative pole; cornice/valance, ruched blinds.
Curtains: full-length, lined drapes in luxury fabrics with feature headings/trims/tassels; diaphanous sheers, lace panels; swags and tails, draped-pole effects.

 FLOORS Theme-enhancing: ceramic tiles; marble; natural wood; color-coordinated carpet; vinyl tile or sheet vinyl.

 BATHROOM FIXTURES Distinctive/period: antique or retro-style bathroom set, freestanding roll-top bath; period fixtures, glass and marble; designer radiators/heated towel rail; formal radiator covers.

 FURNITURE Themed: sophisticated touches with antique-style chairs, chest of drawers or table; dark and dramatic built-in units.

 LIGHTING Adjustable: create atmosphere with dimmer switches; period-style chandelier; streamlined self-colored sconces; candles.

ACCESSORIES Formal/eclectic: ornate gilt or wood mirror; period-style shelves; innovative storage containers; display of collectors' items; dramatic ceramics and glassware; extravagant flower display.

➤ *Sweet and sentimental, a bath entwined with a flowering wisteria bough would appeal to anyone with a romantic spirit. Gentle shades of green, applied as a colorwash to walls and paneling, and the delicately stencil-painted motif, ensure a feeling of restful calm prevails throughout this simple scheme.*

BATHROOM FURNISHINGS

Wallcoverings or paint effects, fabrics, flooring and accessories all play a vital role in the Dramatic bathroom. Each element should have a special quality or contribution to make to the style. For real impact, aim to create bold color and pattern statements with your furnishings, while avoiding an over-fussy or cluttered look which would detract from the finished effect.

You can usually substitute expensive brocades, satin, slub silks and shot metallic materials with less expensive alternatives, such as lining fabrics, bedspreads, throws and antique tablecloths; or "pad out" small amounts of luxury fabric with basics such as toning solids. As generous amounts are often needed to create swathed effects and impressive drapes, furnishing shortcuts make good sense and can look just as effective.

Extravagance is a keynote of the Dramatic style, and antique-style bathroom fixtures and period furnishings help re-create a bygone opulence. Add to this with deep-colored walls and rich furnishings. Bold color contrasts, such as ruby red and forest green or midnight blue and gold, suit this approach, as do lighter, but grand effects using toile de Jouy and glossy chintz. Complement the style with formal window treatments, such as swags and tails or heavy, lined curtains with traditional decorative features, such as goblet headings and tassel trims.

A low-key bathroom only needs an injection of vibrant color to make it dramatically different. A scheme with simple, uncluttered lines, as here, can take an expanse of bold color well. This is balanced by the neutral tones of the painted floor, limed wood paneling and the soft pastel fabrics, and complemented by the splashes of jewel color chosen for accessories.

The theme is mysterious and sensual, with sleek and stylish highlights. Moody shades of amethyst and silver have a glimmering allure – dramatic qualities that are realized and repeated in little touches throughout the scheme; through the silver block print decoration on the walls and roll-top bath, the shiny star mobile and the myriad other metallic glints.

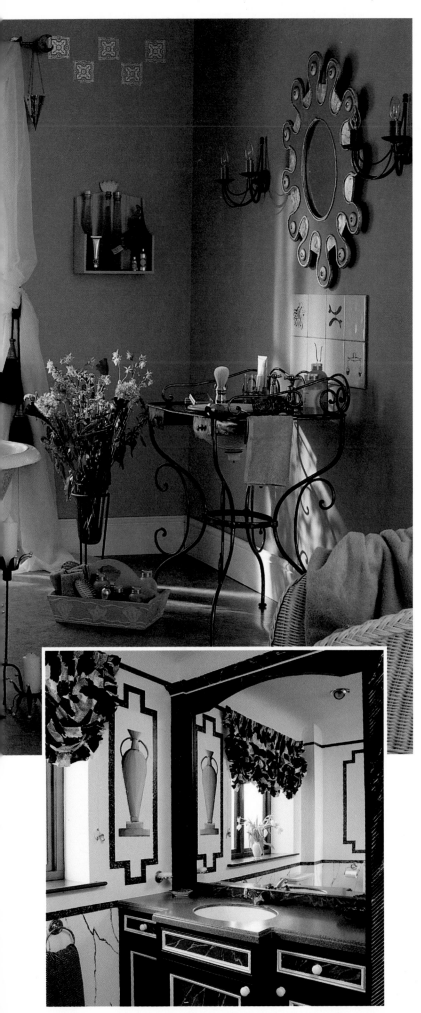

△ *Plush red and forest green, with more than a hint of glinting gold, create a dramatic atmosphere with operatic overtones. The intimate feel created by this type of rich color effect works very well in a small bathroom.*

Appealing to the senses

As Dramatic-style furnishings are designed to appeal to the senses, aim for a scheme that not only looks good but feels good too. Think about combining rough and smooth surfaces; rough plaster walls or a rustic paint effect with smooth tiles; mosaic effects with a fine, smooth wood floor. Combine dark with light; curvy with hard edge; think of the fluid lines of an ornate mirror or picture frame against a strongly colored wall. Team heavily textured fabrics with silky sheers. Introduce chunky shapes and textures through driftwood or dark polished wood furniture. Above all, use color – bombard the walls with vibrant color or a paint effect; add accents with luxury pile towels and elegantly styled accessories. Always look for an opportunity to surprise and delight the eye.

◁ *The impact of black and white is immediate; it presents the most dramatic color contrast you can find, and is a classic combination for creating sophisticated drama. Used in bold sweeps, as here, and with splashes of gray and broken color in the marble effects, mottled textures and fabric print, the effect has a satisfyingly theatrical flourish.*

141

INDEX

Photograph Acknowledgments: Cover Creative Publishing international, 5 Creative Publishing international, 6-7 Eaglemoss/Graham Rae, 8(sp) Eaglemoss/Adrian Taylor, (b) Worldwide Syndication, 9(t) Robert Harding Syndication/IPC Magazines/Country Homes and Interiors, (bl) Robert Harding Syndication/IPC Magazines/Woman's Journal, (br) Eaglemoss/Adrian Taylor, 10(t) Robert Harding Syndication/IPC Magazines/Country Homes and Interiors, (sp) Eaglemoss/Adrian Taylor, (br) Crowson Fabrics, 11-12 Creative Publishing international, 13(t) Hatt Kitchens, (b) Divertimenti, 14-15(c) Elizabeth Whiting and Associates/Brian Harrison, 15(br) Robert Harding Syndication/IPC Magazines/Ideal Home, 16(tl) Bentons Kitchens, 16-17(tc) Robert Harding Syndication/Homes and Gardens/Colin Poole, 16-17(bc) Robert Harding Syndication/Homes and Gardens/Brian Harrison, 17(tr) Hatt Kitchens, (br) Robert Harding Syndication/Homes and Gardens/Fritz von der Schulenberg, 18(tl) Spode, (tr) Paula Rosa Kitchens, (cr) Robert Harding Syndication/Country Homes and Interiors/Polly Wreford, (bl) Creative Publishing international, (br) Houses and Interiors, 19(t) Robert Harding Syndication/Ideal Home/Clifford Jones, (b) Robert Harding Syndication/Homes and Gardens/James Merrell, 20(b) Robert Harding Syndication/Homes and Gardens/Simon Brown, 20-21 Cuisines Schmidt, 22(br) Robert Harding Syndication/Homes and Ideas/Dominic Blackmore, (l) Eaglemoss/Lizzie Orme, 22-23(tr) Robert Harding Syndication/Woman's Journal/Christopher Drake, 23(tr) Robert Harding Syndication/Homes and Gardens/James Merrell, (bl) Creative Publishing international, (br) Robert Harding Syndication/Country Homes and Interiors/Nadia McKenzie, 24(t,c) Creative Publishing international, (b) Eaglemoss Publications, 25(tr) Elizabeth Whiting and Associates/Spike Powell, (b) Robert Harding Syndication/Homes and Ideas/Andreas von Einsiedel, 26-27 Stag, 27(tr) Dulux, (bl) Robert Harding Syndication/Homes and Gardens/Jan Baldwin, 28-29(tr) Robert Harding Syndication/Homes and Gardens/James Merrell, 28-29(b) Elizabeth Whiting and Associates/Rodney Hyett, 29(tr,bl) Creative Publishing international, (br) Elizabeth Whiting and Associates/Rodney Hyett, 30 Creative Publishing international, 31(tr) Robert Harding Syndication/Homes and Gardens/Arthur Hunt, (b) Robert Harding Syndication/Country Homes and Interiors/Jonathan Pilkington, 32 Creative Publishing international, 33 McCord, 34(bl) Creative Publishing international, 34-35(b) Elizabeth Whiting and Associates/Neil Lorimer, 35(tr) Creative Publishing international, (b) Robert Harding Syndication/Country Homes and Interiors/James Merrell, 36(tl) Shaker, (tr) Creative Publishing international, (bl) Elizabeth Whiting and Associates/Spike Powell, (br) Eaglemoss/Graham Rae, 37(tl) Robert Harding Syndication/Ideal Home/Malcolm Robertson, (b) Eaglemoss/James Duncan, 38-39 Robert Harding Syndication/Ideal Home/Dominic Blackmore, 39(b) Marks and Spencer, 40(tl) Robert Harding Syndication/Country Homes and Interiors/Andreas von Einsiedel, (tr) Eaglemoss/James Duncan, (b) Creative Publishing international, 41(tl) Robert Harding Syndication/Ideal Home/Dominic Blackmore, (tr) Eaglemoss/James Duncan, (b) Robert Harding Syndication/Homes and Ideas/Dominic Blackmore, 42 Creative Publishing international, 43(t) Robert Harding Syndication/Homes and Gardens/Christopher Drake, (b) Creative Publishing international, 44-45(b) Robert Harding Syndication/Homes and Ideas/Dominic Blackmore, 45(tr) Elizabeth Whiting and Associates, 46(tr) Robert Harding Syndication/Perfect Home/Brian Harrison, (b) Biggie Best, (br) Robert Harding Syndication/Homes and Gardens/Tim Beddow, 47(t) Elizabeth Whiting and Associates/Brian Harrison, (bl) Biggie Best, 48(tr) Ariadne Holland, (cl) Robert Harding Syndication/Country Homes and Interiors/Simon Brown, (bl) Robert Harding Syndication/Homes and Gardens/Flavio Gallozzi, (br) Eaglemoss/Graham Rae, 49(t) Robert Harding Syndication/Country Homes and Interiors/Tim Imrie, (b) Robert Harding Syndication/Country Homes and Interiors/Christopher Drake, 50 Sanderson, 51(tr) Robert Harding Syndication/Country Homes and Interiors/Christopher Drake, 52(bl) Robert Harding Syndication/Country Homes and Interiors/Jan Baldwin, 52-53(t,b) Ariadne Holland, 53(tr) Robert Harding Syndication/Ideal Home/Dominic Blackmore, 54(tr) Ariadne Holland, (cl) Robert Harding Syndication/Ideal Home/Dominic Blackmore, (cr) Robert Harding Syndication/Homes and Gardens/Jan Baldwin, (bl) IKEA, 55(t) Robert Harding Syndication/Options/Henry Bourne, (b) Robert Harding Syndication/Homes and Gardens/Alex Wilson, 56 Robert Harding Syndication/IPC Magazines/Woman's World, 57 Robert Harding Syndication/Homes and Ideas/Russell Sadur, 58(tr) Robert Harding Syndication/Ideal Home/Di Lewis, (b) Abode Interiors, (b) The Interior Archive/Tim Beddow, 59(tr) Worldwide Syndication, 60(tr) Elizabeth Whiting and Associates/Brian Harrison, (b) Abode Interiors, 61-62 Creative Publishing international, 63(bl) Robert Harding Syndication/Country Homes and Interiors/Andreas von Einsiedel, (r) Elizabeth Whiting and Associates/Brian Harrison, 64 Smallbone of Devizes, 65 Stag, 66(tr) Robert Harding Syndication/Homes and Gardens/James Merrell, (bl) Elizabeth Whiting and Associates/Michael Dunne, 67(tr) Elizabeth Whiting and Associates/Nick Carter, (bl) Robert Harding Syndication/Ideal Home, (tr) Robert Harding Syndication/Homes and Gardens/Brian Harrison, (bl) Dorma, (br) Robert Harding Syndication/Homes and Ideas/Bill Reavell, 69(t) Robert Harding Syndication/Ideal Home/Dominic Blackmore, (b) Biggie Best, 70(t) Elizabeth Whiting and Associates/Andreas von Einsiedel, 70-71 Laura Ashley, 72(bl) Robert Harding Syndication/Ideal Home/Dominic Blackmore, 72-73(t) Abode Interiors, (b) Biggie Best, 73(tr) Coloroll, (br) Robert Harding Syndication/Country Homes and Interiors/Andreas von Einsiedel, 74 Creative Publishing international, 75(tl) Marie Claire Idées/G&C Chabaneix/Hamon, (b) Robert Harding Syndication/Ideal Home/Di Lewis, 76 Arcaid/Lucinda Lambton, 77 Elizabeth Whiting and Associates/Michael Dunne, 78(c) Robert Harding Syndication/Ideal Home/Di Lewis, 78(b) Arcaid/Belle/Geoff Lung, 78-79(t) Robert Harding Syndication/Ideal Home/Di Lewis, 79(tr) Robert Harding Syndication/Country Homes and Interiors/Christopher Drake, (bl) Robert Harding Syndication/Ideal Home/Lucinda Symons, 80(tl) Robert Harding Syndication/Country Homes and Interiors/Bill Batten, (tr) Creative Publishing international, (bl) Robert Harding Syndication/Homes and Ideas/John Suett, (br) Robert Harding Syndication/Homes and Gardens, 81(t) The Interior Archive/Simon Brown, (bl) Eaglemoss/Lizzie Orme, 82 The Interior Archive/Simon Brown, 82-83 Robert Harding Syndication/Homes and Gardens/Simon Upton, 84(tr) Robert Harding Syndication/Homes and Gardens/Elizabeth Zeschin, (bc) The Interior Archive/Wayne Vincent, 85(tr) Robert Harding Syndication/Country Homes and Interiors, (bl) Eaglemoss/Lizzie Orme, (br) The Interior Archive/Simon Brown, 86(tc) Eaglemoss/Lizzie Orme, (tr) Robert Harding Syndication/Homes and Ideas/Dominic Blackmore, (b) Robert Harding Syndication/Homes and Gardens/Simon Upton, (br) Biggie Best, 87(t) Robert Harding Syndication/Options/Simon Upton, (b) Robert Harding Syndication/Homes and Ideas, 88 Abode Interiors, 89 Harlequin Fabrics, 90(cl) Robert Harding Syndication/Homes and Ideas/Bill Reavell, (bc) Robert Harding Syndication/Options/Tom Leighton, 90-91(t) Robert Harding Syndication/Country Homes and Interiors/Lucinda Symons, 91(tr) Robert Harding Syndication/Homes and Ideas/John Suett, (b) The Imrie Tait Partnership/Tim Imrie/Dulux/Homes and Gardens, 92(tl) The Imrie Tait Partnership/Tim Imrie/Dulux/Homes and Gardens, (tr) Robert Harding Syndication/Homes and Ideas/Bill Reavell, (cr) Robert Harding Syndication/Country Homes and Interiors/Simon Brown, (bl) Robert Harding Syndication/Homes and Ideas/Dominic Blackmore, 93 Robert Harding Syndication/Homes and Ideas/Dominic Blackmore, 94-5(c) Robert Harding Syndication/Homes and Ideas/Dominic Blackmore, 95(br) Home Flair Magazine, 96(tr) Robert Harding Syndication/Homes and Ideas/Colin Poole, (b) Robert Harding Syndication/Homes and Ideas/Bill Reavell, 97(t) Biggie Best, (br) Jane Churchill, 98(tl) Next Interiors, (cr) Robert Harding Syndication/Homes and Ideas/Dominic Blackmore, (bl) Robert Harding Syndication/Homes and Ideas/Bill Reavell, (br) Creative Publishing international, 99 Doe Het Zelf Holland, 100(tl) Robert Harding Syndication/Homes and Ideas/Dominic Blackmore, 100-101 International Interiors, 102(t) Robert Harding Syndication/Ideal Home/Malcolm Robertson, (c) Elizabeth Whiting and Associates/Spike Powell, (b) Worldwide Syndication, 103(tr) Creative Publishing international, (bl) Wild Wood, (br) Laura Ashley, 104(t,bl) Robert Harding Syndication/Homes and Ideas/Dominic Blackmore, (br) Creative Publishing international, 105-106 Creative Publishing international, 107 Robert Harding Syndication/Ideal Home/Dominic Blackmore, 108-109 Elizabeth Whiting and Associates/Tim Beddow, 109(br) Elizabeth Whiting and Associates/Dennis Stone, 110(t) Robert Harding Syndication/Ideal Home/Tim Beddow, (br) Robert Harding Syndication/Country Homes and Interiors/Andreas von Einsiedel, 111(tl) Elizabeth Whiting and Associates/Di Lewis, (b) Robert Harding Syndication/Homes and Ideas/Dominic Blackmore, 112 Creative Publishing international, 113(bl) Creative Publishing international, (br) Elizabeth Whiting and Associates/Brian Harrison, 114 Elizabeth Whiting and Associates/Tom Leighton, 115 Robert Harding Syndication/Country Homes and Interiors/Marianne Majerus, 116(cl) Robert Harding Syndication/Ideal Home, (br) Robert Harding Syndication/Homes and Gardens/Steve Tanner, 116-117 Robert Harding Syndication/Country Homes and Interiors/Polly Wreford, 117(tr) Robert Harding Syndication/Ideal Home/Brian Harrison, (br) Robert Harding Syndication/Ideal Home, 118(tr) Eaglemoss/Lizzie Orme, (l) Creative Publishing international, (cr) Robert Harding Syndication/Country Homes and Interiors/James Merrell, 119(tl) Abode Interiors, (br) The Interior Archive/Simon Brown, 120(br) Elizabeth Whiting and Associates/Clive Helm, 120-121 Ideal-Standard, 122(tr) Elizabeth Whiting and Associates/Andrew Kolesnikow, (bl) Robert Harding Syndication/Homes and Gardens/Tim Beddow, (br) Elizabeth Whiting and Associates/Steve Hawkins, 123(tr) Elizabeth Whiting and Associates/Steve Hawkins, (b) Elizabeth Whiting and Associates/Nick Carter, 124(tr) The Interior Archive, (c) Robert Harding Syndication/Homes and Gardens/Debi Treloar, (bl) Robert Harding Syndication/Homes and Gardens/James Merrell, 125(t) Ideal-Standard, (b) Eaglemoss/Laura Wickenden, 126, 127 Sottini, 128 Doulton, 129(tr) Doulton, (b) Sottini, 130(tr) Robert Harding Syndication/Homes and Ideas/Ian Skelton, (cl,br) Next Interiors, 131 Creative Publishing international, 132-133 Robert Harding Syndication/Country Homes and Interiors/Christopher Drake, 133(tl) Robert Harding Syndication/IPC Magazines/Brock, 134(tr) Elizabeth Whiting and Associates, (bl) Abode Interiors, 135(tl) Eaglemoss/Graham Rae, (tr,b) Abode Interiors, 136(tr) Abode Interiors, (tr,br) Creative Publishing international, (bl) Eaglemoss/Graham Rae, 137 Abode Interiors, 138-139 Robert Harding Syndication/Country Homes and Interiors/Christopher Drake, 139(tr) Robert Harding Syndication/Homes and Gardens/Christopher Drake, 140(bl) Robert Harding Syndication/Country Homes and Interiors/Polly Wreford, 140-141 Robert Harding Syndication/Homes and Ideas/Dominic Blackmore, 141 Elizabeth Whiting and Associates/Brian Harrison.

Creative Publishing international offers a variety of how-to books. For information write:

Creative Publishing international
Subscriber Books
5900 Green Oak Drive
Minnetonka, MN 55343
1-800-328-3895